1976

be kept

FOURTEEN DAYS

ok is kept overtime

A
LITERARY
HISTORY
OF
SPAIN

A LITERARY HISTORY OF SPAIN

General Editor: R. O. JONES
Cervantes Professor of Spanish, King's College, University of London

THE MIDDLE AGES
by A. D. DEYERMOND
Professor of Spanish, Westfield College, University of London

THE GOLDEN AGE: PROSE AND POETRY
by R. O. JONES

THE GOLDEN AGE: DRAMA
by EDWARD M. WILSON
Professor of Spanish, University of Cambridge
and DUNCAN MOIR
Lecturer in Spanish, University of Southampton

THE EIGHTEENTH CENTURY
by NIGEL GLENDINNING
Professor of Spanish, Trinity College, University of Dublin

THE NINETEENTH CENTURY
by DONALD L. SHAW
Senior Lecturer in Hispanic Studies, University of Edinburgh

THE TWENTIETH CENTURY
by G. G. BROWN
Lecturer in Spanish, Queen Mary College, University of London

SPANISH AMERICAN LITERATURE
SINCE INDEPENDENCE
by JEAN FRANCO
Professor of Latin American Literature, University of Essex

CATALAN LITERATURE
by ARTHUR TERRY
Professor of Spanish, The Queen's University, Belfast

A LITERARY HISTORY OF SPAIN

THE EIGHTEENTH CENTURY

A LITERARY
HISTORY OF SPAIN

THE EIGHTEENTH
CENTURY

NIGEL GLENDINNING

Professor of Spanish, Trinity College,
University of Dublin

LONDON · ERNEST BENN LIMITED

NEW YORK · BARNES & NOBLE INC

First published 1972 by Ernest Benn Limited
Bouverie House Fleet Street London EC4A 2DL
and Barnes & Noble Inc. 49 East 33rd Street New York 10016
(a division of Harper & Row Publications Inc.)
LC# 72-186206
Distributed in Canada by
The General Publishing Company Limited . Toronto

Printed in Great Britain

ISBN 0 510-32271-9

ISBN 0-389-04619-1 (USA)

Paperback 0 510-32272-7

Paperback 0-389-04620-5 (USA)

860.9
B558

CONTENTS

73616

FOREWORD BY THE GENERAL EDITOR

SPANISH, the language of what was in its day the greatest of European powers, became the common tongue of the most far-flung Empire the world had until then seen. Today, in number of speakers, Spanish is one of the world's major languages. The literature written in Spanish is correspondingly rich. The earliest European lyrics in a post-classical vernacular that we know of (if we except Welsh and Irish) were written in Spain; the modern novel was born there; there too was written some of the greatest European poetry and drama; and some of the most interesting works of our time are being written in Spanish.

Nevertheless, this new history may require some explanation and even justification. Our justification is that a new and up-to-date English-language history seemed called for to serve the increasing interest now being taken in Spanish. There have been other English-language histories in the past, some of them very good, but none on this scale.

Every history is a compromise between aims difficult or even impossible to reconcile. This one is no exception. While imaginative literature is our main concern, we have tried to relate that literature to the society in and for which it was written, but without subordinating criticism to amateur sociology. Since not everything could be given equal attention (even if it were desirable to do so) we have concentrated on those writers and works of manifestly outstanding artistic importance to us their modern readers, with the inevitable consequence that many interesting minor writers are reduced to names and dates, and the even lesser are often not mentioned at all. Though we have tried also to provide a usable work of general reference, we offer the history primarily as a guide to the understanding and appreciation of what we consider of greatest value in the literatures of Spain and Spanish America.

Beyond a necessary minimum, no attempt has been made to arrive at uniform criteria; the history displays therefore the variety of approach and opinion that is to be found in a good university department of literature, a variety which we hope will prove stimulating. Each section takes account of the accepted works of scholarship in its field, but we do not offer our history as a grey consensus of received opinion; each contributor has imposed his own interpretation to the extent that this could be supported with solid scholarship and argument.

Though the literature of Spanish America is not to be regarded simply as an offshoot of the literature of Spain, it seemed natural to link the two in our history since Spanish civilisation has left an indelible stamp on the Americas. Since Catalonia has been so long a part of Spain it seemed equally justified to include Catalan literature, an important influence on Spanish literature at certain times, and a highly interesting literature in its own right.

The bibliographies are not meant to be exhaustive. They are intended only as a guide to further reading. For more exhaustive inquiry recourse should be had to general bibliographies such as that by J. Simón Díaz.

R.O.J.

PREFACE

THE TEXT of this book was originally intended as a contribution to a larger volume including the Romantic and post-Romantic periods. It is obviously impossible to do justice to more than a hundred years of Spanish literature in such a relatively short space, and I have preferred to restrict the number of authors discussed rather than to bring in writers merely for the sake of mentioning them. I hope nevertheless that these chapters may contribute to the wider understanding of an era which was once severely neglected, but which is now increasingly the object of scholarly research in France, the United States, Germany, Italy and Spain, as well as in these islands.

A number of colleagues and friends gave me timely advice when I was working on books published by subscription in Spain and investigating book prices. I am more particularly indebted to the late Professor Antonio Rodríguez-Moñino, now sorely missed by Hispanists everywhere, and to Professor Edward M. Wilson; also to Mrs Helen F. Grant, Professor José Caso González, Mr Duncan Moir, and Professor Russell P. Sebold. I am also grateful to many students of Spanish at the University of Southampton who helped me to check statistics, and to the University authorities who generously financed some of my research. I gratefully acknowledge the permission of the Trustees of the British Museum, and the Biblioteca Nacional, Madrid, to reproduce quotations from manuscript material in their collections. I also acknowledge that, unless otherwise stated, English versions of Spanish originals, whether manuscript or printed, are my own. Finally I must express my gratitude to the General Editor of the series, Professor R. O. Jones, for his careful scrutiny of my typescript and for bringing some of its shortcomings to my notice in time. Thanks are also due to my wife for removing some of the many infelicities of my prose, and to Philip Deacon who prepared the index and helped me check the proofs.

Dublin   O.N.V.G.
June 1971

LIST OF ABBREVIATIONS

AHN	Archivo Histórico Nacional
BAE	*Biblioteca de Autores Españoles*
BBMP	*Boletín de la Biblioteca de Menéndez Pelayo*
BH	*Bulletin Hispanique*
BHS	*Bulletin of Hispanic Studies*
BNM	Biblioteca Nacional, Madrid
BRAH	*Boletín de la Real Academia de la Historia*
CA	*Cuadernos Americanos*
CC	Clásicos castellanos
CCa	Clásicos Castalia
CCF	*Cuadernos de la Cátedra Feijoo* (Oviedo)
FR	*Filología Romanza*
HR	*Hispanic Review*
NBAE	*Nueva Biblioteca de Autores Españoles*
NRFH	*Nueva Revista de Filología Hispánica*
PSA	*Papeles de Son Armadans*
RABM	*Revista de Archivos, Bibliotecas y Museos*
RCHL	*Revista crítica de historia y literatura*
RFE	*Revista de filología española*
RH	*Revue Hispanique*
RL	*Revista de Literatura*
RLC	*Revue de Littérature Comparée*
RN	*Romance Notes*
SPh	*Studies in Philology*

Note. The dollar equivalents given in Chapter 1 and Appendix B are at the rate of $2.40 to the pound sterling.

Chapter 1

LITERATURE AND SOCIETY IN EIGHTEENTH - CENTURY SPAIN

SPAIN WAS A DIVIDED COUNTRY at the beginning of the eighteenth century. Castile supported the Bourbon candidate for the throne, Philip V; while the old kingdom of Aragon wanted the Archduke Charles. After the end of the war Philip gave the Aragonese some motives for continuing their opposition, by abolishing the special privileges (*fueros*) of Aragon, Valencia, and Majorca in 1716. The Aragonese faction was still a force to be reckoned with in the 1760s and 1770s, and there were other groups at that time trying in Spain, as elsewhere in Europe, to modify the old hierarchies of monarchy and Church. But divisions were not the only consequence of the War of the Spanish Succession. By the treaties of Utrecht and Radstat, Spain lost the Spanish Netherlands, Naples, and Sicily to Austria; Gibraltar and Minorca to the British. The country was as Voltaire and other eighteenth-century writers said, a skeleton of its former self.

When Ferdinand VI became king in 1746, the politician Macanaz used a similar cadaverous image to describe the state of the nation. He blamed the interference of foreign advisers in Spanish affairs as well as the wars. Although there had been a distinct improvement in the Spanish economy, and population was on the increase, there was a strong sense that Spain was in decline. Further improvements later in the century still failed to remove entirely the smell of decay.

The government solutions to the problem were initially economic: the removal of the internal customs barriers, the protection of certain industries—like glass, porcelain, shipbuilding, and cloth—repopulation of the Sierra Morena region in the late 1760s and early 1770s, and official support for the Economic Societies which sprang up, after a lead from the Basques in 1765 in all the major centres. The very existence of these Economic Societies reflected a wide concern for

1

the country's development. They were formed by individuals who wanted to improve the agricultural and commercial efficiency of the country, and were mostly composed of rich people trying to encourage progress in manual work in which they were not actively engaged themselves, according to a satirist of the period (*El Censor, Discurso* 65, Madrid, 1781).

Other people sought social and political solutions to Spain's problems. In the later part of the century complaints against the idleness of the upper classes were particularly common, and these were reinforced by an awareness of the changes taking place in the structures of other societies. Some felt that the situation would be improved by breaking 'the links which bound wealth to certain persons and certain organisations, instead of to the industrious, the persevering, and the meritorious' (*El Censor, Discurso* 9, Madrid, 1781). The poet and dramatist Cándido María de Trigueros, in one of his *Odas filosóficas* in the 1770s, felt that legal measures would be in order against the idle rich, arguing the case in persuasive rhyming couplets:

> The dwellers of the Nile in ancient times
> would punish idleness like other crimes.
> Solon dispatched the drones to foreign lands;
> the lazy soon were killed at Draco's hands.
> The Germans too paid idleness with death,
> and in their muddy bogs stifled its breath.
> The voice of Reason praised in all these states
> the Spanish nobleman vituperates.
> Meanwhile we, with misplaced pride and pleasure,
> give our feudal lords a life of leisure.
> Their famous forebears' lives of useful work
> bequeath their sons, it seems, the right to shirk.
> And now, a futile burden on the nation,
> their only function is self-admiration.

These criticisms of a useless aristocracy, sometimes linked to the egalitarian attitudes which were very much in the air in the late eighteenth century, are readily understandable in the context of Spain. The proportion of nobles in Spain was not high, and it declined in the course of the century until it was a mere 4 per cent of the total population of 10½ million in 1797. In the census of 1768 there were 722,794 *hidalgos*; 480,000 in 1787; and 403,000 in 1797. But in certain areas the proportion of nobles was greatly in excess of the proportion over the country as a whole. Guipúzcoa, exceptionally, was 100 per cent *hidalgo*; Vizcaya 50 per cent and Asturias 16 per cent at the end of the century. Furthermore, although the percentage of nobles per head of population was low in Andalusia, *hidalgos* there were particularly rich. Over the country as a whole nobles still enjoyed considerable privileges. They did not pay the 'pecho' tax and were exempt from torture. In Madrid there was a special meat supply for nobles in the Plazuela del Salvador (without purchase tax), and another for ordinary people (with tax) in the Plazuela de San Ginés. In many parts of the country whole towns, as well as villages and lands, still belonged to virtually autonomous overlords, rather than to the crown or the Church. Vast tracts of cultivable soil were wasted as a result of neglect by absentee landlords, and as a result of the entailing of estates, or unusable because they belonged to the sheep and cattle-owning organisation called the Mesta, which had rights to land on either side of the sheep- and goat-trails leading across Spain from summer to winter pastures. In the *Informe sobre la ley agraria* (1795), written by Jovellanos (1744-1810) on the basis of discussions and papers of the Economic Society of Madrid, the redistribution of land and the encouragement of wider ownership were felt to be urgent necessities. But not all wanted such radical change, and Bernardo Ward in 1750 had thought that the establishment and Spain could be saved together by reintroducing the silk industry, so that villagers would breed worms and spin, and landowners invest their hoarded money, in a material that clothed the aristocracy or draped palace walls.

To some extent wars, as so often in Spanish history, impeded the country's development. The retaking of Naples and the kingdom of the Two Sicilies in 1734; an expensive campaign in Italy between 1740 and Philip V's death in 1746; war with England in Portugal in 1762; a raid on the Falkland Islands in 1770; a disastrous attack on Algiers in 1775; the siege of Gibraltar between 1779 and 1783; the recapture of Minorca in 1782; hostilities against the new French republic from 1793 to 1795; and subsequently the Peninsular War (1808-14): all these cost money and men that Spain could ill afford. It is true that in some instances national pride was at stake and war made for unity. But in some cases war was merely the result of

alliance with France—particularly after the Family Pact of 1761-62—
and in others a source of humiliation, as in the calamitous raid on
Algiers. The Peninsular War both divided and unified Spain at one
and the same time. Liberals were divided amongst themselves, not
knowing whether it was better to support France in the long-term
interest of their country, because that was more likely to bring
radical change in Spanish society, or to support Ferdinand VII
against the French and try to exact from him a more democratic
system than the Spanish monarchy had previously provided. Ultimately the end of the war saw an impoverished nation and the
restoration of absolute monarchy despite the Constitution of Cadiz
(1812).

War inevitably sharpened the Spanish concern for Spain's state
and status, and certainly much was done in the eighteenth century,
despite hostilities, to improve her situation. The conditions of life in
towns were radically altered, with cobbled streets, better drains, and
lighting at night in the capital; new avenues and squares everywhere;
model suburbs at Barcelona (Barceloneta); and model towns built by
enlightened individuals (that of the Goyeneche family at Nuevo
Baztán) and by the state (La Carolina and La Carlota and others in
Andalusia). Communications throughout the country were greatly
improved, and new highroads and canals were planned and constructed in the second half of the century. Advances in agriculture
and industry were encouraged, as was the study of mathematics and
the sciences—to teach Reason and eradicate superstition. An
attempt was also made by the government in the 1770s to reform the
universities and improve school-teaching.

No changes come without opposition and division. In the eighteenth
century reforms which affected the Church were particularly divisive.
In some respects they have to be seen in the light of a struggle for
power between two rival monarchs, King and Pope. Whether
criminals could claim sanctuary from the secular arm in churches;
whether the Pope had the authority to depose kings or free a king's
subjects from their obligations to the monarch; whether the clergy
could appeal to civil authorities against apparent abuses of ecclesiastical powers; and whether the Church had the right to publish
papal edicts without the permission of the king: these were all hotly
debated questions. Those who attacked the power of the papal curia
were accused by the Church of Jansenism or threatened by the

Inquisition. In return the king's Ministers sought to diminish the power of the Holy Office, ban certain papal edicts, and undermine organisations whose allegiance lay too clearly with the Pope. The expulsion of the Jesuits in 1767 was seen as a major blow in the battle against the curia. Ten years later the trial by the Inquisition of Olavide, a Minister imbued with Enlightenment ideas and a driving force in the plan to repopulate the Sierra Morena region, showed that the war was not yet over. Towards the end of the century many issues became confused as a result of this struggle for power. A churchman like Joaquín Villanueva, who spoke out against the way in which some clergy said mass—a twelve-minute mass was not unusual at the time and some ecclesiastical greyhounds ran it in a breathless five—was as likely to be imprisoned by the Inquisition as was an atheist. On the other hand the Church could sometimes seem a natural ally for democrats in the struggle against the absolute power of the crown.

Advanced thinkers of all persuasions had problems with the Inquisition in Spain throughout the century. For most inquisitors the sun and stars still went round the earth; even in the 1770s Copernican theory was as much of a heresy in Olavide's trial as were lack of respect for religious images or sensualist ideas. According to the Benedictine writer Padre Feijoo in the 1720s, the Inquisitor-General was a diehard then ('amantísimo de la antigualla'), and though some later ones were not, works had to be amended so as not to upset the Inquisition if they were to be printed. The banning of a book was an incentive to some to read it, but the inquisitors were feared by artists and writers and used by the government after 1789 to prevent the spread of revolutionary ideas.

The progressive decline in the number of inquisitorial trials and punishments in the eighteenth century can be followed in the figures given by J. A. Llorente (1756-1823) in his *Memoria histórica* (1811), recently republished by Editorial Ciencia Nueva under the title *La Inquisición y los españoles*. The figures are slightly impressionistic. Llorente had figures he believed to be accurate for some tribunals, but multiplied these by the number of other tribunals in the country to get a global figure. For the purposes of comparison, however, his figures are consistent enough for statistical analysis. From them it is possible to note three periods of significantly intense activity: namely, the years 1711-18, 1742-45, and 1793-97. The first of these coincides with the Wars of Succession and their aftermath, the second with wars in Italy, and the third with the post-French Revolution period. Llorente gives figures for each of the reigns of the various Inquisitors-General, and I have added these together where practicable to divide the periods as nearly into decades as possible. Some Inquisitors-General, however, lasted for more than ten years, and where there is a serious disparity between the number of years covered by one reign and the next I give a corrected figure in brackets. This is appropriate for comparison with the immediately preceding reign only.

Years	1699-1710	1711-18	1720-33	1733-40
Persons burnt	204 ?	272	442	238
Burnt in effigy	102 ?	136	221	119
Punished	1,224?	1,632	2,652	1,428
Total	2,810	2,040 (2,958)	3,305 (1,518)	1,785

Years	1742-45	1746-59	1760-74	1774-83
Persons burnt	136	10	2	2
Burnt in effigy	68	5	—	—
Punished	816	107	10	16
Total	1,020 (2,346)	122	12	18

Years	1784-92	1793-97	1798-1808
Persons burnt	—	—	—
Burnt in effigy	—	—	1
Punished	14	30	20
Total	14	30	21

After 1760, according to Llorente, more individuals were examined in secret and not subjected to public indignities or confiscation of property. There was, therefore, more activity than might appear from the figures in the second half of the century.

The government censors also helped to preserve religious as well as state institutions from attacks in print. After widespread riots in 1766 and again after the French Revolution they were particularly vigilant, and in 1793 a group of intellectuals who wanted to publish a periodical called *El Académico* made a promise which shows the power of censorship over the press at that time. 'We will say nothing, quote nothing, and become involved in nothing which might cause offence' they claimed, 'and would rather pass for ignorant in the eyes of some than for men of new ideas'.

Government censors and Inquisitors might keep much of the Enlightenment out of print; they could not keep it out of Spain. In the 1770s the bishop of Plasencia complained to the king of the ease with which he had procured the irreligious and subversive writings of Voltaire himself. If such works could not be published in Spain, it was difficult to avoid their discussion at private gatherings (*tertulias*), and in coffee-houses. In 1776, Padre José Rodríguez wrote in *El Philoteo*:

> There can be no doubt whatever that there are now and have been in the past *tertulias* attended by officers, ladies, and other personages whose chief subject of conversation is fashionable religious ideas. Doubts are expressed about purgatory, Hell, the immortality of the soul, divine revelation, the supreme authority of Church and state, and everything leads to dissolute ways and the life of the libertine.

Some satirists of the period suggested that you could not get on in Spanish society without a smattering of the Enlightenment. This was in part the burden of José Cadalso's *Los eruditos a la violeta* (Madrid, 1772), and the anonymous manuscript attack on Olavide called *El siglo ilustrado* (*c.* 1778). It was the whole point of an anonymous sonnet of the same period which runs more or less as follows:

> I believe in the doctrines of Voltaire,
> worship the Kouli Khan and the Turkish Spy.
> The Inquisitors on whom I most rely
> are Montesquieu, Rousseau and D'Alembert.
> I shout aloud that Spain sore needs repair.
> Her stock of superstition, though, is high.
> Nollet's, Descartes' and Newton's wares I cry;
> time for Lord Bacon's name I'll always spare.
> Monks, friars and nuns receive my constant taunts,
> products I'll praise of any foreign state;
> Naples and Paris are my favourite haunts;
> with mistress rather than with wife I mate.
> And since I lard with French words all I say,
> official posts are bound to come my way.
>   (British Museum, Add. MS. 10, 257 f 309 v)

This satirical poem was probably aimed at Spain's foreign advisers and Ministers, who were familiar with Enlightenment ideas, as well as at those Spaniards who adopted modish attitudes to gain advancement. It was perhaps in the tradition of Macanaz's attack on influential foreigners at the Spanish Court earlier in the century; an attack which was repeated by the rioters in 1766 who sought the removal of Charles III's Italian Minister Esquilache. At that period, as earlier, the deep divisions and resentments of Spanish society came to the surface. Charles III and his new Minister, the conde de Aranda, attempted to heal some of the breaches by expelling the Jesuits (on suspicion of involvement in the riots). The policy pursued was basically to strengthen central authority, as it had been at the beginning of the century.

In the field of the fine arts and literature centralisation worked by creating a network of academies. More particularly from the 1740s onwards,[1] these ensured that the provinces accepted the architectural styles and artistic standards approved at Court: basically the styles of Greece and Rome and the European Renaissance, called at this period Neo-classicism. New work in provincial churches needed the approbation of Madrid from November 1777,[2] and the Real Academia de San Fernando was constantly being asked to vet new plans and developments. Although local fashions by no means disappeared, they were less inevitably adopted by Spanish artists than had previously been the case.[3] A similar move towards standardisation took place in language and literature. The dictionary on which the Real Academia Española embarked soon after its creation in 1714 helped to give greater uniformity to language, while the censors appointed by the Academies guaranteed the style and literary (as well as political and religious) purity of works whose publication they authorised. In Spain, in fact, there is evidence to support the contention that the spread of Neo-classicism was a reflection of enlightened despotism. But the unified values of the main teaching orders also aided and abetted this aesthetic doctrine by educating the young in Horace and Aristotle.

Although Spain was a more united country in the middle of the eighteenth century she was also more closely linked to the rest of Europe than she had been for some time. The new Bourbon dynasty made for cordial relations with France, but there were important political ties with England (and Ireland) and Italy too, and these had cultural as well as economic consequences. French painters, sculptors, and landscape gardeners, Flemish weavers and Italian architects worked for Philip V; Ferdinand VI continued the tradition; and Charles III brought Giovambattista Tiepolo and the Bohemian Mengs to Madrid to work in the royal palaces and churches. The china-factory Charles had set up at Capodimonte outside Naples with Italian artists was moved virtually lock, stock, and barrel to the Buen Retiro in Madrid when he succeeded to the throne in 1759. The musical taste of the country was also modified as a result of wider European contacts in the course of the century.

Italian opera dominated the Court from the 1720s to the 1750s. Alessandro Scarlatti worked for the Spanish in Naples, and his son Domenico wrote much of his music in Spain, dying in Madrid in 1757. In 1737 the famous castrato Carlo Broschi (Farinelli) came into the Spanish royal service with a princely salary of 1,500 English guineas a year. Having eased Philip V's melancholia—the king 'imitated Farinelli, sometimes air after air' according to Sir Benjamin Keene, the English ambassador—he went on to sing duets with Bárbara de Braganza, the wife of Ferdinand VI, organising the operatic spectacles in the Buen Retiro during the latter's reign. Charles III was less personally amenable to music—Italian or other-wise—and on his accession popular feeling, voiced in anonymous poems and counting the cost of the previous reign, required Spanish reforms in music, as well as in five other areas beginning with M: medicine and Ministers, mules, modes and 'mujeres'. Charles's brother the Infante Don Luis, however, supported both Spanish and foreign musicians, playing organ duets with Padre Soler, and taking Boccherini on his staff. Furthermore, a music printing-house, set up in Madrid in 1770, published works by composers of international standing as well as those of Spaniards.[4] Yet it should not be assumed that there was an entirely one-way traffic of art and music into Spain. Haydn wrote the *Seven Last Words from the Cross* for Cadiz cathedral; the Valencian-born composer Vicente Martín y Soler (1754-1806) had an opera performed in Vienna in 1786 from which Mozart took a theme for *Don Giovanni*, and was director of the Italian opera in St Petersburg when he died. And if the Bohemian Mengs painted a number of Spanish aristocrats in the middle of the century, Goya was later to paint the French ambassador Guillemardet and the duke of Wellington, and sold a number of early copies of his *Caprichos* to foreign buyers.

Literature was obviously affected by the increasing awareness of foreign theory and practice. Writers like Luzán or Juan de Iriarte who were educated in Italy and France, or like Cadalso who travelled widely in Europe and studied in London and Paris, had a first-hand knowledge of European literature. Others, like Jovellanos and Meléndez Valdés who learned foreign languages in Spain and had French, English, and Irish contacts there, were equally widely read in foreign authors. Frenchmen and Italians residing in Spain—like Ignacio Bernascone who was educated at a school in Getafe, and the San Fernando Academy, or Conti and Napoli Signorelli who lived in the capital for some years[5]—clearly stimulated interest in foreign literature in the circles they frequented, and publications of Spaniards who had travelled abroad no doubt helped to spread the interest to a wider public. Leandro Fernández de Moratín clearly gave pride of place to cultural matters in the notes he made—perhaps with a view to publication—when travelling in England and Italy;[6] and Luzán in 1751 and the duque de Almodóvar thirty years later passed on to the reading public in Spain the impressions they formed of French culture during periods of residence in Paris: the former in his *Memorias literarias de París: Actual estado y método de sus estudios* (Madrid, 1751), the latter in the *Década epistolar sobre el estado de las letras en Francia* (Madrid, 1781) by 'Francisco María de Silva'. Travel was not limited to the upper classes, however, since there were royal pensions and scholarships to help Spanish craftsmen and artists to study in England, France, and Italy. The growing study of foreign languages in Spanish schools[7] also enabled more people to read French, English, and Italian works in the original and broaden the impressions they received in some instances from translations. But the influence of translations in style as well as in content should not be underestimated. Capmany maintained in the late 1770s or early 1780s that these had largely transformed the way Spanish was written in a matter of twenty years,[8] though many would say that the change was for the worse.

The importance of social change in Spain has already been indicated. The government itself, for economic reasons, had an interest in breaking down some of the traditional status barriers. Campomanes tried to encourage the development of the crafts by raising their social status and by challenging the distinction between the Dons who practised the liberal arts and the plain Juan Fernándezs who worked at looms, lasts, or lathes. From March 1783, crafts like tanning, tailoring, shoemaking, and ironwork were declared 'honour-able', and those who practised these trades did not lose their *hidalguía* by so doing.[9] Yet the status-structure died hard. The desire to be rated as *Don* was clearly a reality and not just a figment of Cadalso's imagination in the 1770s, when he wrote about *Donimania* in the *Cartas marruecas,* and the distinction he makes between *Don* and *Señor Don,* is plainly to be seen in the subscription-list for Sancha's edition of Lope's *Obras sueltas* in 1776[10]. Furthermore, changes at the centre did not always bring about the desired changes at the periphery. The Real Academia de San Fernando was still complaining in 1784 about provincial demarcation disputes between artists and craftsmen, and despairing about the closed-shop attitudes adopted by guilds of painters in Majorca, Catalonia, Saragossa, and Valencia.[11]

It took the Peninsular War to make the first real breach in the status system, when non-*hidalgos* became officers. Nevertheless, even small changes in social patterns have clear implications for literature, and these, together with improvements in school facilities offered at the period,[12] lead us perhaps to assume too rapidly that the reader-ship for literature widened in the course of the century. It is easy to postulate the emergence of a new lower middle-class reader, and to expect a new kind of writer to develop for a new sort of public.

Unfortunately there are no reliable sources of information about the public for books in Spain in the eighteenth and early nineteenth centuries. The lists of subscribers to books published by subscription may perhaps, however, give some indication of likely trends. Admittedly subscribers were not necessarily readers, and Torres Villaroel, who claimed that the Salamanca 1752 edition of his *Obras* was the first Spanish work to be published by subscription, speaks of his supporters as 'persons who out of pity, piety, or curiosity have subscribed to a copy of these works'.[13] Yet an analysis of seventeen volumes published in Spain between 1752 and 1817 seems to reflect a decline in subscribers at the uppermost end of the social scale over the period in question (see below, Appendix A). This should not be taken to indicate a radical shift to a less establishment or less 'upper-class' readership and patronage for literature, however. The shift in that direction is gradual, minute perhaps, in the eighteenth century, though not totally insignificant. Most books in Spain continued to be written by nobles or *hidalgos* for nobles and *hidalgos*. The difference was perhaps in the fact that the *hidalgo* element was now increasingly gainfully employed on what the nineteenth century would call 'middle-class' pursuits: international commerce, the wholesale trades, and banking, as well as the traditionally *Don* professions of army, the Church, medicine, university, law, and civil service.

If the social context of literature was changing, what of the publication itself? The most obvious change here was in the supply and demand for various categories of book. Most of the basic research on the subject remains to be done, and Spain badly needs the equivalent of the French *Livre et société dans la France du XVIIIᵉ siècle* (2 vols., Mouton, Paris, 1970). From the few sources readily available it is clear that there was a significant rise in the percentage of scientific, medical, and economic books printed in the early nineteenth century, reflecting clearly the impact of the Enlightenment in that area. It is also clear that literature accounted for a relatively small proportion of publications. In 1815, to judge from announcements of books in the *Gaceta de Madrid*, religious books had the highest percentage with about 22 per cent. Yet this is very much lower than the percentage published eighty-five years earlier in 1730 when the figure was 52 per cent. The total number of books printed increases fourfold over the same period. A small rise is found in educational books and in history and geography; also in political publications. The percentage of periodicals falls from 13 to 2 per cent between 1760 and 1815, and printings of Latin and Greek authors also decline from 4 per cent to just under one per cent. (See below Appendix D.)

Another significant change in books in the eighteenth century was in the quality of the product. Both the paper and type improved vastly in the second half of the century. Printers learned from France and tried to compete with other European countries; certain of them —like Ibarra and Sancha—set high standards which other Spaniards tried to follow. Earlier in the century publications were often of very poor quality, and matters were not always helped by the tendency of authors to use local printers. Many works which seem of key importance today were in fact printed in the provinces. Luzán's *Poética*, for example, was printed on extremely poor paper in Saragossa in 1737 —'villanamente impreso' as Padre Isla put it;[14] the first edition of the *Orígenes de la poesía castellana* by Luis José Velázquez, the marqués de Valdeflores, came out in reasonably presentable form from the town of his birth, Málaga, in 1754; and Mayans y Siscar, who lived in Oliva near Valencia, generally used his local presses too.

The particular problem about the use of local printers was that they did little to encourage circulation, which depended on the initiative of writers. Padre Isla's recipe for getting his books known was to send complimentary copies to friends in cities where a new publication of his was to be sold.[15] The theory was that the friends would stimulate sales. Often, however, distribution was only really ensured by reprinting, not always with the author's permission.

How many copies of books can have made even the journey from Madrid to Catalonia if the Sancha edition of Cadalso's *Cartas marruecas* (Madrid, 1793) had to be copied almost line for line by Piferrer and published in Barcelona only three years after it first appeared? If the bookselling trade had been well organised this would hardly have been necessary. Indeed, Padre Isla's letters are full of bitter complaints about the inefficiency of agents. Publishers began to make greater efforts to push their productions at the end of the eighteenth century, however, and often included lists of their books at the back of publications at that time. In 1786 Juan Sellent listed twelve works available from the Librería of the Viuda de Piferrer, and thirty on a longer list published in 1790.[16] Separate catalogues from publishers and booksellers are also a feature of the period. And an analysis by five-year periods of the dated or datable catalogues listed by Rodríguez-Moñino in his study of booksellers' catalogues[17] shows the same trend towards increased publicity for literature at the end of the century. There is a total of twenty-two catalogues in the fifty-five years between 1725 and 1780 (with peaks in 1745-50 and 1775-80); thirty-seven between 1780 and 1805 (with a peak in the 1790s); sixty-four between 1805 and 1830 (with an obvious highpoint in the 1820-25 period); and forty-five between 1830 and 1850. Examination of a small sample suggests that the number of books announced in each was also on the increase at the same period. Another sign of improved efficiency in the book trade is the change in style of book advertisements in the *Gaceta de Madrid*. These chiefly reported the booksellers in Madrid from whom new publications could be obtained in the eighteenth century, whereas in the nineteenth provincial booksellers handling the publication tend to be noted too.

Equally relevant to the question of book circulation is the size of editions. Evidence here suggests that there was little increase over the practice of previous centuries during most of the eighteenth century. The standard seventeenth-century edition seems to have numbered 1,500 to 1,750 copies, and similar figures crop up in the eighteenth century too. Sancha printed 1,500 copies of his edition of *Don Quixote* in 1777[18], a work which was constantly in demand. Ibarra printed the same number of P. Jerónimo Rosales's immensely popular *Catón cristiano* in 1755, although this was supposed to be an advance on an edition of 40,000 in all.[19] Although Padre Isla wanted an edition of three thousand to be made of the first part of his *Fray Gerundio de Campazas* in 1758, only 1,500 were in fact ordered by his publisher, and second impressions of other Isla works seem to have been of the same modest size.[20] Three thousand copies were certainly printed of volumes 5 and 6 of Feijoo's *Teatro crítico universal*, but this seems to have been rather exceptional.[21] And in Moratín's play *La comedia nueva* Don Serapio's wildest dreams of successful sales of *El cerco de Viena* are only 'more than eight hundred copies',[22] suggesting once again an edition of between one and two thousand copies in all.

If 1,500 copies remained the standard size of an edition, there is some evidence that smaller editions still were made in the eighteenth century. Can fifteen hundred copies of Cadalso's *Los eruditos a la violeta* have been printed in 1772, if the whole edition was sold out (bar twenty-seven copies) before the work's publication was announced in the *Gaceta de Madrid*? Would the 141 subscribers to Juan de Iriarte's *Obras sueltas* (Madrid, 1774) have wanted as many as ten copies each of the work to give to friends? Certainly not more than 800 copies were made of Tomás de Iriarte's didactic poem *La música* when it was printed with the backing of the conde de Floridablanca in 1779[23].

An edition of fifteen hundred copies seemed small to some printers, however, in the late 1780s. The editor of a new edition of the *Obras* of Fernán Pérez de Oliva (Madrid, 1787) wrote that copies of the 1585 edition were rare 'since no more than 1,500 copies were printed which have inevitably vanished after two hundred years'.[24]

The size of editions naturally has to be seen in relation to the probable size of the reading public. According to the 1768 census Spain had between 9 and 10 million inhabitants, and it seems likely that about 70 per cent of these would have been unable to read or write. That was the level of illiteracy at the end of the nineteenth century and there is no reason to suppose that the percentage was any lower a hundred years previously. Perhaps, then, there were between one and two million possible readers in the whole of Spain in the middle of the eighteenth century. In a city like Madrid, which had a total population of 167,607 inhabitants in 1797—not much bigger than Reading or Huddersfield in England today—there may well have been only 50,000 readers in all. Consequently, although wide circulation was obviously rare in eighteenth-century Spain, those who were interested soon heard about new publications. It is extraordinary, for instance, how well known certain works became which were not printed at all and which circulated in manuscript copies. This was more particularly the case of works which were unlikely to pass the censors without serious dilution for political or religious reasons. Moratín's *Arte de las putas*—philosophically justified with some wit by the author on the grounds that it is morally better to write about love than war—was well known in the author's circle and widely enough read to merit listing in the Inquisition's Index of prohibited books. The satire on Pablo de Olavide and the passion for French culture in Spain entitled *Vida de Don Guindo Cerezo* also circulated freely in manuscript in the late 1770s. Anonymous political satires, like the articles of the *Duende de Madrid* during the reign of Philip V, and the *Testamento de España* in the time of Ferdinand VI, were widely read in manuscript; and so, it appears, was the parody *Calendario manual* attributed to Cadalso in 1768, which upset the more amorous members of the aristocracy who did not want the names of their current lovers and mistresses to be broadcast at Court.

Circulation, however, is only one of the writer's problems, and we must now consider the extent to which the economics of book-publishing provided incentives or deterrents. Some books were commissioned by academies or Patriotic Societies and published at their expense, and of course a rich man could always afford his own printing costs and publish what he liked. But most authors were not commissioned to write and depended then, as now, on the generosity of publishers, the vagaries of public taste, and, occasionally, on moneylenders. Certain printers in the second half of the century appear to have launched minority-appeal works at their own expense. Antonio Sancha claims (on the title page!) that he was doing this when he published Vicente García de la Huerta's *Obras poéticas* in two volumes in Madrid in 1778. It was Sancha too who backed the publication of Jovellanos's *Informe sobre la ley agraria*, when the Madrid Economic Society, officially responsible, was short of funds in 1794.[25] Authors whose publications were not financed by a printer or a generous Maecenas sometimes seem to have relied on advances from booksellers, while others appear to have borrowed money from merchants, as was the case of the dramatist Ignacio López de Ayala, who paid interest on his repayments of the order of 7 per cent.[26]

Pressures on the writer in the eighteenth century, then, were hardly negligible, as Cadalso admitted when he defined five classes of European writer in *Carta* LXVI of his *Cartas marruecas*. According to him there were those who wrote whatever they wanted; those who wrote what others told them to write; those who said the opposite of what they felt; those who set out to please and flatter the public; and those who set out to shock the public and criticise it. There would have been few in the first and last categories in Spain, and only those in the second and fourth will have made anything out of their writing. Yet there is some evidence that useful money was beginning to be made by authors. According to Don Hermógenes in *La comedia nueva* a dramatist could expect to earn 'fifteen doubloons' from a play's performance in the 1790s.[27] This was the equivalent of £12 in English money at the period, and was quite a large sum; about £150 ($360) or more at today's prices.

But you had to please the public fairly assiduously to live by the pen alone, and the only documented case at the period is that of Francisco Mariano Nipho (1719-1803). Nipho essentially published what the public wanted—periodicals, translations, popularising works—yet only after sacrificing his stomach and clothes to print, in the 1760s and 1770s ended up solvent. A catalogue entirely dedicated to his publications appeared late in the century, and he was then able to buy his son a commission in the army and provide annuities for both his son and his daughter on the proceeds of his writing.[28]

Given these economic circumstances, it is clear that the number of writers who could actually live by the pen in Spain in the eighteenth century was minimal. To earn money in some other way, to have a profession, or to have a protector, were then as now the paths normally open to the writer. The playwright Cañizares had an appointment in the household of the duques de Osuna, and even a

dramatist as enormously in demand as Ramón de la Cruz, who also
had a civil service post, needed to be 'kept'.[29] Huerta worked in the
Royal Library for a living; Meléndez Valdés as university professor
and lawyer; Tomás de Iriarte was a civil servant; Cadalso a cavalry
officer; Leandro Fernández de Moratín an official translator.

Yet if the author's freedom was limited to some extent by his
financial circumstances, so was that of his reader. How far did the
cost of books and the price of theatre tickets restrict the public for
literature?

A change in the economics of both books and plays seems to have
taken place in the 1760s. Before that time official machinery for pric-
ing books (the *tasa*) ensured that there was little variation in their cost
to the consumer. In the first half of the century there was a more cr
less standard rate of 6 or 8 *maravedís* for each gathering, and much
the same price index had obtained in the late seventeenth century.[30]
Prices appear to have risen, however, when the *tasa* was abolished by
Royal Order of 14 September 1762. A copy of Padre Joseph Núñez
de Prado's *Gramática de la lengua francesa* (Madrid, 1760) in the
author's possession had its price fixed at 117 *maravedís* on publication, yet a manuscript note on the fly-leaf shows that it was sold by
a bookseller called Cubillas on Wednesday in Holy Week, 1764, for
7 *reales*. This represents a price rise of 3 *reales* and 19 *maravedís*,
or over 50 per cent, in under four years. In Spain, in fact, books of
any length were financially as well as intellectually beyond the reach
of any but the upper-class readers. Torres Villarroel's relatively short
Vida (1743) only cost 60 *maravedís* (4½d. [2p.]; 5 cents), but Luzán's
Poética (1737) sold for 768 *maravedís* (5/0¼d. [25p.]; 60 cents), and
the first part of Isla's *Fray Gerundio* (1758) for 336 *maravedís*
(2/2½d. [11p.]; 26½ cents). The set of the Spanish *Enciclopedia
metódica* (1782-94) was 200 *reales* (£2 4s. [£2.20]; $5.28), and
Meléndez Valdés valued his copy of Montesquieu's *L'Esprit des lois*
at 127 *reales* (£1.8.2d. [£1.41]; $3.38), and the *Oeuvres philo-
sophiques* of Diderot at 100 *reales* (£1.2.2d. [£1.11]; $2.66). Equiva-
lents must be multiplied from ten to fifteen times to give some idea
of their relative cost today. A more detailed breakdown of book prices
is given below in Appendix B.

As for the theatre, it was not really much more accessible. All
prices were increased by a *cuarto* in August 1770; 'entrada' was
2 *reales* (5d. [2p.]; 5 cents), the patio 3, and most other seats 6 *reales*

2 * *

(about 6p. or 14 cents) in January 1771. Boxes came to 30 or 47 *reales* (upwards of 6/8d. [33½p.] or 80 cents), and an 'aposento segundo' was 22 *reales*. The poorer classes could rarely afford to go. Alonsillo in Ramón de la Cruz's *Deseo de seguidillas* would have liked to see a play, but it would cost 'una peseta' (4 *reales*) for the patio, a sum which would provide him with lunch for two. A peseta was about a sixth of a servant's monthly salary (25 *reales*), according to Cruz's *La pradera de San Isidro*, and a farm labourer normally earned only 6 *reales* per day.

For the poorer members of the reading public, however, there were at least some new incentives at the end of the eighteenth century and the beginning of the nineteenth. Printers tried to encourage more people to buy books by offering sets on economic subscription terms, and facilities for lending books or reading them in libraries or reading-rooms were extended at the same period. The Biblioteca Real had opened as early as 1712, and copies of all new books had to be given to the library. Sempere y Guarinos wrote that the Biblioteca Real 'is full of the best Spanish books which anyone is allowed to read',[31] and he attributed considerable importance to the library's role in the development of literary taste and knowledge in Spain. Lending libraries run in conjunction with bookshops do not seem to have opened to the public until after the Peninsular War, and their real impact was on the readership of the Romantic period. Faulí in Valencia published a catalogue 'of books available for subscribers to read' around 1817 and Cabrerizo followed suit ten years later in the same city.[32] Joaquín Adrián produced a catalogue of the contents of his 'Gabinete de lectura' in Seville in 1837 and a number of 'gabinetes' were advertised in the Madrid newspapers between 1833 and 1842.[33] Readership of periodicals was particularly encouraged in this way. Entry to reading-rooms seems to have cost 2 *cuartos* for one periodical and four to read the lot. Alternatively there was a monthly subscription rate of 8 *reales*.

Even if there were not any facilities in most cities in Spain in the eighteenth century for the borrowing of books except from private individuals, the growth of the periodical itself at that period obviously enabled some writers to reach a wider public, including some of those who may not have been able to avail themselves of even the cheaper books.[34] Some publications, like the *Diario de los literatos de España* (1737-42), made important contributions to the discussion of literary theory, and contributed much to the establishment of Neo-classical principles in Spain. Others, like *El Censor* and the *Correo de Madrid*, were important as vehicles for the ideas of the Enlightenment. But the influence of periodicals on writers as well as readers deserves some consideration.

Two literary forms, which in the eighteenth century were often closely linked to the periodical, were the short essay—sometimes informative, sometimes satirical—and the letter. These were not so much forms created by periodical literature, as readily adaptable to it. Another pre-periodical form which was to become a staple of periodicals in Spain in the late eighteenth century and the early nineteenth was the fictional dream or *sueño*. From the amply proportioned *Dreams* of Quevedo and his eighteenth-century imitator Torres Villarroel, the *sueño* was compressed to fit into the pages of the *Correo de Madrid* and the leaves of Goya's *Caprichos*, and later expanded again (although still within the ambit of periodical literature) by Larra in the 1820s and 1830s. Periodicals encouraged the development of short forms, controversy and polemic, anonymity or pseudonymity in writers, rapid and even casual reading habits in readers. Writers who catered for periodical readers clearly had to bear this in mind; and Nipho (who rarely catered for any other type of reader) even went so far as to italicise the philosophical *sentencias* in his translation of the marqués de Caracciolo's *Viaje de la razón por Europa* to catch the eye of the rapid reader of the period.[35]

Whatever the effect of periodicals on the style of writing in the eighteenth century, their effect on the circulation of certain works of literature cannot be doubted. Cadalso's *Noches lúgubres* was printed in two separate periodicals before it came out in book form; and the same author's *Cartas marruecas* circulated first in the *Correo de Madrid* before the publication of Sancha's edition in 1793. Jovellanos's 'Sátira segunda a Arnesto sobre la mala educación de la nobleza' was first printed (in a bowdlerised version in *El Censor*) in May 1787 before reaching another public in García de Arrieta's *Principios filosóficos de la literatura de Charles Batteux* in 1801 and final publication as a separate in 1814. Other poems by Jovellanos of a satirical nature first saw the light in the *Diario de Madrid* in 1788 and 1797,[36] and Meléndez Valdés, presumably by arrangement with Jovellanos, published his poetic *Discurso* on the moral and material decadence of Spain a week before the 'Sátira segunda a Arnesto' in

El Censor. Meléndez printed other poems in the *Correo de Madrid*, the *Diario de Madrid*, and the *Semanario erudito y curioso de Salamanca*, and two of his *Discursos forenses* were first published in 1818 in the *Almacén de frutos literarios*;[37] his friend Forner brought out some translations of Horace and a dialogue in the *Diario de las musas* in Salamanca.[38] Further evidence of the attractiveness of the periodical for Spanish writers in the second half of the eighteenth century is provided by Nicolás Fernández de Moratín's decision to publish selections of his poems in that form in the 1760s (*El Poeta*), and Clavijo y Fajardo's choice of the same form for his satirical essays (*El Pensador*, Madrid, 1762-67). The periodical passion also moved Trigueros in the 1770s to publish his philosophical poems at intervals rather than as a single group; and the passion becomes a mania in some minor writers of the period, to judge from the case of Lucas Alemán y Aguado, chief editor of the *Correo de Madrid* and author of at least eighty-four volumes of manuscript ephemera.[39]

If periodicals encouraged some new reading and writing patterns, other patterns also existed which must have affected the way in which people wrote. Not all people read rapidly, and the common practice of reading aloud meant that books did not always have the unity we expect from them today. It is not surprising that the beauties of individual lines of poetry, or passages of prose, were as important to the eighteenth-century reader and writer as the impact of a poem or book as a whole. In a letter to his friend Carlos González de Posada, dated 5 May 1792, Jovellanos lays down strict rules for the writing of musically balanced lines of poetry. The practice of reading aloud may have led writers to favour shorter forms, and easily fragmentable larger structures; it certainly encouraged the use of aural effects in prose as well as verse. Prose, in fact, is synonymous with eloquence at the period; 'Obras de elocuencia' *means* works in prose.

So far our prime concern has been with changes of environment and readership in the eighteenth century, and with external factors affecting the form and style of literary expression. We must now look at two other forces affecting Spanish writers: the impact on Spaniards of foreign aesthetic theory, and their reactions to foreign and national views of Spanish culture.

Spain's sensitivity about her image abroad has often been the subject of comment. If she worried about her declining political power in Europe in the seventeenth and early eighteenth centuries, it was only natural that she should also worry about the international standing of her literature at the same period. As early as 1609 Quevedo had reacted strongly to slights on Spain and her literature— above all her supposed propensity to an inflated and impure style— from writers like Marc-Antoine Muret and Scaliger.[40] Eighteenth-century Spaniards were decidedly more defensive when dealing with similar attacks. It was more difficult perhaps for eighteenth-century defenders of Spanish literature to hold up recent writers as examples of Classical control. While Quevedo could turn to Luis de León, Garcilaso, Luis de Granada, Herrera, and many others, the eighteenth century turned to Solís occasionally, but more usually to the same sixteenth-century writers as Quevedo, and to seventeeth-century proponents of Classicism like Cascales, José Antonio González de Salas, the brothers Argensola, the condes de Fernán-Núñez, and Rebolledo.

Typical of late seventeenth-century criticism of Spanish literature by foreigners, which eighteenth-century Spaniards tried to meet or refute, is that of the Père Bouhours's *Entretiens d'Ariste et d'Eugène*. This French Jesuit only really approved of his own language. Spanish in his view,

> fait pour l'ordinaire les objets plus grands qu'ils ne sont et va plus loin que la nature; car elle ne garde nulle mesure en ses métaphores; elle aime passionnément l'hyperbole et la porte jusqu'à l'excès, de sorte qu'on pourrait dire que cette figure est la favorite des Castillans.[41]

Other writers, like Montesquieu or Saint-Evremond, shot wittier bolts but bolts nevertheless. The former implied that the only good Spanish book (*Don Quixote*) criticised all the others; the latter traced the supposed irregularity and lack of naturalness of Spanish style back to the Moors.[42] It was inevitable that Spaniards should feel they were under fire. And the fire persisted into the middle of the eighteenth century and beyond. In May 1748, a review of Luzán's *Poética* in the *Mémoires pour l'histoire des sciences et des beaux arts* maintained that since the early seventeenth century Spain had hardly produced a single work 'écrit d'un stile raisonnable'; and in the same year a map of Spain with four headings appeared in a work published in Avignon, which declared that the country was largely uninhabited, useless, a breeding-place for monsters, and the ruination of 'all good literature'.[43]

These adverse comments on Spanish culture acquired still wider currency in Europe when Masson de Morvilliers asked the famous question 'Que doit-on à Espagne?' in the *Encyclopédie méthodique*. His article on Spain was completely rewritten and the irony expunged in the Spanish translation published in Madrid by Sancha (1782-94), but the original attack became widely known and continued to provoke Spaniards understandably for more than a hundred years. A spate of counter-attacks followed, some of them so vituperative that the Council of Castile refused to grant a licence to print in at least one instance.[44] Sempere y Guarinos's replique was a bold assertion of the high standards of his Spanish contemporaries. Juan Francisco de Masdeu (1744-1817) an exiled Jesuit, on the other hand, spent much time defending Latin writers who had lived in Spain at the time of the Romans and barely got round to discussing Spanish literature at all in the twenty volumes of his *Historia crítica de España y de la cultura española*. Manuel Benito Fiel de Aguilar felt that the complete answer to foreign attacks was a Spanish translation of Nicolás Antonio—'the catalogue or library of the most notable men the nation has produced in all branches of learning'.[45] Capmany's reply to Spain's critics—the *Teatro histórico-crítico de la elocuencia española*—rather undermines Aguilar's case, however, since it attributes much of the foreign criticism to ignorance of the Spanish language.

In the 1780s and 1790s, however, Spaniards were confident enough to hit back at foreign critics. The situation sixty years earlier had been very different. Most Spanish intellectuals had then felt that the criticism of Spanish literature could be substantiated, and their response to attacks was to try to improve the ground they had to defend. In 1725 Mayans y Siscar complained about Fray Félix Hortensio Paravicino's imitators 'whose only concern has been for the meaningless sound of high-flown words, saying much yet signifying nothing'; he also inveighed against the abuse of 'poetical phrases' in Spanish.[46] Luzán (1702-54) made similar points in his *Poética* (Saragossa, 1737), although he deplored the 'indecorous expressions' of critics like Bouhours.[47] In the middle of the century Spaniards almost despaired of finding a way to defend their culture. Montiano y Luyando, in 1753, referred to 'the need to vindicate our nation, which has always been the chief end of my efforts',[48] and a decade later, Clavijo y Fajardo, at the start of the third *Pensamiento* of his periodical *El Pensador*, wondered whether there was any way to overcome 'the boldness of foreigners who mock us to our very faces'. One obvious way of answering foreign criticism was to try and make Spanish taste conform with that of other European countries. Bouhours and the marqués de Valdeflores offered new aesthetic criteria and a reassessment of sixteenth-century Spain as the Golden Age of Spanish literature; Montiano y Luyando set an artistic example by writing tragedies to prove that Spaniards were capable of following Classical principles.

Gradually, as confidence in Spain's ability to produce literature which other countries would respect returned, Spanish writers began to revalue their past in a more assertive manner. Calderón's theatre as a whole still had few defenders, yet the ideas expressed in it found a clear admirer in Forner.[49] And although Góngora's long poems were usually deplored by critics, his shorter poems were acclaimed, and Herrera began to be held up as an example of Spanish qualities in poetry, whose passion and fire were preferable to the chill precision of French poetry and its Spanish imitators.[50] Cienfuegos, and the poets of the Sevillian school like Lista, Reinoso, and Blanco White, were his strongest advocates. As relations with France worsened in the 1790s, criticism of French literary values became more common in Spain, and was particularly violently expressed by even earlier admirers like Capmany at the time of the Peninsular War. Another reason for the reappraisal of 'irrational' Spanish writers was the growing interest in the Sublime in literature in the second half of the eighteenth century. There was also a new advocacy for 'national' rather than 'international' styles, reaching a climax after the Peninsular War when the theories of A. W. Schlegel began to circulate in Spain.

New aspects of foreign aesthetic theory began to have an impact in Spain at the time. Reference has already been made to the growing Spanish awareness of European Neo-classicism before 1760, yet there appears to have been a swing away from French criteria in the second half of the century. Even in Luzán's *Poética*, French theory had only been one element in a broad spectrum.[51] Meléndez Valdés's library, though certainly heavily weighted with French books, balanced Père André, Batteux, Boileau, Diderot, Marmontel, and Du Bos with Aristotle, Horace, Hutcheson, Mengs, Pope, and Shaftesbury. Two translations of Boileau's *Art poétique* were certainly published in Spain (by Madramany and Arriaza) in 1787 and 1807, and one of Batteux's *Principios filosóficos* . . . (9 vols., Madrid, 1797-1805). Yet these were balanced by Munárriz's translation and compendium of Hugh Blair which ran into eight editions between the end of the century and 1824, and Juan de la Dehesa's translation of Edmund Burke's *Treatise on the Sublime* (Madrid, 1807). The *Espíritu de los mejores diarios* brought English and German as well as French material to its public in the 1780s and 1790s, and so did the continuation of the *Memorial literario* under the editorship of José Calderón de la Barca from 1789.[52] Italian aesthetics also gained ground in Spain at the same period. Sempere y Guarinos (1754-1830) published a free translation of Muratori's *Reflexiones sobre el buen gusto en las ciencias y en las artes* (Madrid, 1782), and Sánchez Barbero's *Principios de retórica y poética* (Madrid, 1805 and 1813) made prominent use of Filangieri as well as of Marmontel. Spanish Jesuits who were exiled to Italy after 1767 contributed greatly to the spread of non-French aesthetic theory. Padre Andrés's (1740-1817) monumental *Historia de todas las literaturas* has much on the poetic theory and practice of Italy, Germany, and England, to say nothing of Russia and other European countries. Estéban de Arteaga's (1747-99) *Investigaciones filosóficas sobre la belleza ideal* (Madrid, 1789) draws ideas from Winckelmann, Sulzer, Mengs, Hagedorn, Algarotti, and Moses Mendelssohn, as well as from André, Crouzat, Voltaire, Marmontel, and Batteux.

Nor should the central importance of Classical and Spanish theory and practice be forgotten. Its influence almost certainly outweighed that of foreign writers with a very high percentage of Spanish authors. The grounding in literature given in Spanish schools was still essentially Latin. The humble pupils of the Escolapian fathers, in their classes of poetry and rhetoric, learned Horace's *Ars poetica* by heart. The more upper-class pupils of the Jesuit seminaries used the same text; and the tradition still persisted when Javier Burgos was examined in Rhetoric and the young Zorrilla in Humanities at the Real Seminario de Nobles in Madrid in 1829.[53] The chair in literary criticism established at the Reales Estudios de San Isidro in 1770 by Charles III seems to have concentrated on Classical and pre-Classical times, and the 'discourses' spread over the first year of the four-year course for those enrolling in 1789 covered 'the culture of the barbarians and the Egyptians, Greeks and Romans up to the decline and fall of the empire'.[54] Translations of Classical authors and theorists were also numerous and important. Estala published Sophocles' *Oedipus tyrannus* (1793), and Aristophanes' *Plutus* (1794), and José Goya y Muniain produced a new version of Aristotle's *Poetics* (1798). Manuel Pérez Valderrábano and Padre Basilio de Santiago translated Longinus' *Treatise on the sublime* (1770 and 1782), and Sancha reprinted Alonso Ordóñez das Seixas's *Poetics of Aristotle* (1778) with Heinsius's and the Abbé Batteux's notes, and José Antonio González de Salas's *Nueva idea de la tragedia antigua*.

Republications of sixteenth- and seventeenth-century Spanish writers also helped to form as well as reflect eighteenth-century taste. Some authors, like Calderón, Lozano, and María de Zayas, were reprinted to meet a known demand which had nothing to do with the development of Neo-classicism. But the more Classical sixteenth- and seventeenth-century writers who filled the nine volumes of the *Parnaso español*, first published by Ibarra and Sancha between 1768 and 1778,[55] were intended to provide examples of 'good taste'. Similar criteria lay behind Azara's edition of Garcilaso (1765), and a series of Spanish classics published under the general editorship of Ramón Fernández (Padre Estala) which included volumes of poetry by Herrera, Jáuregui, and the brothers Argensola. The anacreontics, *sáficos-adónicos*, and *latinas* of Villegas, also republished at the time, were enormously influential, and combined Classical form and elegance with sensuality in a way which particularly appealed in the eighteenth century.

These republications both reflected and moulded the literary taste of the eighteenth century. In the case of Villegas it is clear that an interest in the poet led to his republication; Luzán and Luis José Velázquez had praised him, and Nicolás Fernández de Moratín and Cadalso imitated him before the edition of 1774, republished by Sancha in 1797. Cándido María de Trigueros's *Poesías de Melchor Díaz de Toledo* (Seville, 1776) merely continued this tradition. On the other hand, one may wonder if Pedro Montengón would have written his pastoral novel *Mirtilo* (Madrid, 1795) if a renewed interest in the pastoral novels of Montemayor, Gil Polo, and Cervantes, had not been reflected in reprintings at the period.

Not all influential reprints, however, fall strictly within the bounds of Classical taste, and it is interesting to note that some antiquarian publications also had their impact on literature. A literary counterpart to the archaeological interests of the period and research in the early history of Spain, is the increased interest in pre-sixteenth-century poetry: epics like the *Cid*, the poems of Berceo and the Arcipreste de Hita. Luis José Velázquez was the first to quote extensively from the Archpriest in his *Orígenes de la poesía castellana* (1754), some time before the work's publication in Tomás Antonio Sánchez's *Colección de poesías castellanas anteriores al siglo XV* (Madrid, 1779-90). In the early 1770s or late 1760s Nicolás Fernández de Moratín and Cadalso both tried their hands at poems in old Spanish, either following Velázquez or perhaps imitating Quevedo's *romance* 'Estando en cuita y en duelo'.[56] Jovellanos also uses the same idiom momentarily in some of his own poems, although by the time he was writing a taste for medieval things had established itself in a number of European countries as well as in Spain. Strawberry Hill Gothic in architecture, and Ossian in poetry, were the English manifestations of this taste; and although Gothic remained a term of abuse in Spain, Ossian had some success in translation. One volume of his work translated by Alonso Ortiz came out in 1788 and some translations by Pedro Montengón were published twelve years later.[57] Further interest in these areas may well have been awoken by references in the *Espíritu de los mejores diarios*;[58] Juan Andrés's *Origen, progresos y estado actual de toda literatura* (Madrid, 1784-1806; preceded by Italian editions in Parma, 1782-99, and Venice, 1783-1800); and the *Historia literaria de la edad media*, extracted by a Frenchman from J. Harris's *Philological Inquiries* and published in Spanish in 1791.

Parallel in importance for the Spanish writer to the impact of foreign and Spanish aesthetics, its theory and practice, was the European Enlightenment. New conceptions of law, belief in the experimental sciences above all others, scepticism in religious matters and in history, reached the minority in Spain who were capable of obtaining and reading foreign publications. However, some broad changes of attitude to the Enlightenment took place in Spain in the second half of the eighteenth century. Voltaire and Rousseau were almost unmentionable names in print in Spain from the 1760s onwards, yet Voltaire's plays were translated and performed and some of his short stories printed;[59] and Rousseau's *Discours sur l'inégalité* was widely discussed. Luzán sought to make some of the ideas of the *philosophes* accessible in his *Memorias literarias de París* (Madrid, 1751). But the Esquilache riots in 1766 seem to have caused a more restrictive attitude to the Enlightenment on the part of the government, and after the French Revolution censors and Inquisitors redoubled their activities.[60] A Spanish contemporary of liberal persuasions, Valentín de Foronda, maintained that innovatory ideas in Spain came more and more under pressure after 1789: from that time onwards the stranglehold on thought was progressively tightened. Two years before the Revolution, the dramatist Leandro Fernández de Moratín movingly summarised the dilemma of the Enlightened writer in Spain in the following terms:

> If a Spanish writer repeats what others have said, he is ignored; if he fights against generally accepted ideas, the clergy, breviary in hand, are quick to argue with him, and after a very few syllogisms he can find himself in prison—and God knows when or how he will get out of that. The age in which we live is very unfavourable to us: if we drift with the stream and speak the language of the credulous, foreigners make a mock of us, and even in our own country some people will think us fools; and yet, if we try to sweep away the dangerous errors of the past and teach the ignorant, the Holy Inquisition will give us its usual medicine.[61]

Traditional forms of expression have to be taken into account, as well as traditional ideas, in any survey of the Spanish writer's environment in the eighteenth century, and this brings us to popular literature: ballads and *seguidillas* more particularly were the staple diet of the ordinary people and they did not have to be able to read to assimilate them. The intelligentsia's attitudes to ballads and chapbook literature in general were more ambivalent. Some types of ballad—more particularly the *romances* about criminals like Francisco Esteban and other *guapos*—met with strong criticism because of their supposedly bad moral influence on those who read them or heard them recited or sung.[62] Historical ballads, on the other hand, and even some of the novelesque variety, provided eighteenth-century writers like Huerta, Cadalso, Iglesias, and Jovellanos and Meléndez, with stories to elaborate in their own particular way. It was not until the early years of the nineteenth century that ballads began to be admired as the poetry of the people,[63] but their poetic quality was certainly recognised by the Neo-classics, and their form was used to new political and satirical ends by Meléndez and Jovellanos. Popular *cantares* were also admired for their poetic quality by serious writers.

León de Arroyal in the prologue to his *Epigramas* (Madrid, 1784) quotes three which he claims to have heard very recently and which seemed to him on a par with Classical poetry for wit and beauty. Attitudes to short popular poems of this non-narrative kind seemed to have changed in the early nineteenth century in the same way as attitudes to ballads. When publishing his two-volume *Colección de las mejores coplas de seguidillas, tiranas y polos* (Madrid, 1816), 'Don Preciso' felt they were ideal expressions of the Spanish national spirit, and an appropriate antidote to foreign music—particularly Italian opera 'which cannot do otherwise but make us soft and effeminate'.

Between these two poles—the concern for universal artistic standards and European culture on the one hand, and national traditions on the other—Spanish writers over the whole period inevitably oscillate.

NOTES

1. The dominance of the Madrid Academy through its training of provincial craftsmen is apparent from *Los registros de matrícula de la Academia de San Fernando de 1752 a 1815*, preliminar, transcripción y ordenación por E. Pardo Canalís (Madrid, 1967); it is also evident in some *Reales Resoluciones*. See, for example, Severo Aguirre, *Prontuario alfabético y cronológico por orden de materias, de las instrucciones, ordenanzas, reglamentos, pragmáticas y demás reales resoluciones no recopiladas, expedidas hasta el año de 1792 inclusive* (Madrid, 1793), pp. 9-10 ('Arquitectos').

2. ibid., p. 367.

3. A clear example of a surviving local style is the Neo-Baroque stucco work of Pedraxas in churches in Priego (Córdoba) dating from the 1770s, very much in the Andalusian tradition.

4. See N. Glendinning, 'Influencia de la literatura inglesa en España en el siglo XVIII', *CCF*, 20 (1968), 52.

5. See for Bernascone's education at Getafe the *Memorial ajustado de la causa criminal* . . . *contra D. Benito Navarro* (Madrid, 1768), f 14 v, and in the San Fernando Academy *Los registros de matrícula* . . . , p. 16. On the Italians in general see Vittorio Cian, *Giovambattista Conti e alcune relazioni letterarie fra l'Italia e la Spagna nella seconda metà del settecento* (Turin, 1896).

6. A column inch analysis of the content of Moratín's *Apuntaciones sueltas de Inglaterra* (*Obras póstumas*, Madrid, 1867, I, 161-269), carried out by three Southampton students, suggests that between 35 per cent and 43 per cent of the work relates to the theatre and the arts; 7 per cent to 9 per cent to the sciences, 22 per cent to 28 per cent to 'costumbres', and 10 per cent to 17 per cent to political and economic material.

7. See N. Glendinning, op. cit., 66, and Ángel González Palencia, 'Notas

sobre la enseñanza del francés a fines del siglo XVIII y principios del XIX', in *Eruditos y libreros del siglo XVIII* (Madrid, 1948), pp. 419-27.

8. J. Sempere y Guarinos, *Ensayo de una biblioteca española de los mejores escritores del reinado de Carlos III* (Madrid, 1785), II, 142.

9. Severo Aguirre, op. cit., pp. 11-12.

10. Lope de Vega, *Obras sueltas* (Madrid, 1776), I, Lista de subscriptores.

11. Real Academia de San Fernando, Juntas ordinarias, Libro III (1776-85)—Junta del 5 de diciembre de 1784. Any Spanish or foreign artist or architect was allowed to work freely in Spain at the period, as was reaffirmed in a *Real Cédula* of 1 May 1785 (cf. Severo Aguirre, op. cit., p. 10).

12. The priority which the government gave to the teaching at the period of 'primeras letras' can be seen in the *Real Resolución del 11 de julio de 1771*. There had been regulations for *maestros* since 1758, and free schools were started in all the *barrios* of Madrid in 1783. Provincial capitals were expected to follow suit. For the reform of university education at the same period, see F. Aguilar Piñal, *Los comienzos de la crisis universitaria* (Madrid, 1967), and the same author's *La universidad de Sevilla en el siglo XVIII* (Anales de la Universidad hispalense, serie: Filosofía y Letras, No. 1, 1969).

13. Torres Villarroel, *Obras* (Salamanca, 1752), I, f ¶ ¶ 2 r. Torres refers to the motives of subscribers as 'piedad, por su diversión' in Vol. XIV of the collection, p. 173.

14. Padre Isla, *Cartas inéditas*, ed. P. Luis Fernández (Madrid, 1957), p. 134 (*Carta* No. 134).

15. ibid., p. 192 (*Carta* No. 182).

16. The short list is on the last page of the Barcelona, Viuda Piferrer edition of Cadalso's *Ocios di mi juventud* authorised on 12 December 1786. The *Optica del Cortejo* attributed to Cadalso and published by the same Barcelona press in 1790 has the longer list at the end.

17. A. Rodríguez-Moñino, *Historia de los catálogos de librería españoles (1661-1840)* (Madrid, 1966).

18. Cf. A. Rodríguez-Moñino, 'El *Quijote* de Don Antonio de Sancha', in *Relieves de erudición* (Madrid, 1959), pp. 277-88, especially p. 286.

19. See Á. González Palencia, 'Joaquín Ibarra y el juzgado de imprentas', in *Eruditos y libreros del siglo XVIII*, pp. 330, 344.

20. Padre Isla, *Cartas inéditas*, ed. cit., p. 190 (*Carta* No. 182). References to new impressions of 1,500 copies in *Carta* No. 93, p. 91.

21. See *BAE*, 141, p. xii, note 3.

22. See *La comedia nueva*, Act II, Scene ii. Doña Agustina guesses that 500 copies will have been sold.

23. Hipólito Ricarte was paid for 'cincuenta manos de papel' to be used for printing six plates for the edition. Taking a *mano* as a quire (24 sheets) this would give 400 copies if two plates were printed on each sheet, and 800 if four were printed. The latter seems the most likely since the book is in quarto. (See E. Cotarelo y Mori, *Iriarte y su época*, Madrid, 1897, p. 203.)

24. ibid., I, prólogo del editor. On numbers of copies printed in the seventeenth century see J. O. Crosby, *The Sources of the Text of Quevedo's 'Política de Dios'* (New York, 1959), p. 5, and Francisco Rico's introduction to *La novela picaresca española* (Barcelona, 1967), I, lxxxix, xc.

25. See letter from José de Guevara Vasconcelos to Jovellanos dated 4 October 1794, *BAE*, 86, p. 191.

26. Ayala borrowed 18,604 *reales* from Don Pedro de Zubiaga to cover printing costs of his Spanish translation of the Council of Trent, and agreed to repay 20,000 *reales* in monthly instalments of 500 *reales*.

27. See *La comedia nueva*, Act I, Scene vi. Ramón de la Cruz appears in the late sixties and seventies to have earned 300 *reales* for a *sainete* (£3 6s. 8d.; $7.99) and 1,500 *reales* (£16 13s. 4d.; $40) for his opera *Briseida* and for a play *La toma de Jerusalén* (see E. Cotarelo y Mori, *Don Ramón de la Cruz y sus obras*, Madrid, 1899, pp. 108, 111, and 121). His annual salary as an 'oficial tercero' was 5,000 *reales* (£55 10s.; $133.20), raised later on his promotion. According to Joseph Townsend it was possible for a country parson in Catalonia to live extremely well on £80 ($192) per annum. Cruz could obviously live less well on his salary in Madrid. Yet Moratín only earned 3,664 *reales* or £40 14s. ($97.68) in 1782.

28. See Luis Miguel Enciso Recio, *Nipho y el periodismo español del siglo XVIII* (Valladolid, 1956), *passim*, but especially pp. 8-20.

29. See E. Cotarelo y Mori, op. cit., especially chapters 8, 9, and 12.

30. There seems to have been a steady rise in book prices in the course of the seventeenth century, to judge from a small sample of *tasas*:

1601   Mateo Alemán, *Primera Parte de Guzmán de Alfarache*, Madrid. 3 *maravedís* per *pliego*.

1605   Juan de Solórzano Pereira, *Diligens et accurata de Parricidii crimine disputatio*, Salamanca. 3 *maravedís*.

1641   Félix de Arteaga, *Obras póstumas divinas y humanas*, Madrid. 4½ *maravedís*.

1642   Diego López, *Declaración magistral sobre las sátiras de Iuuenal*, Madrid. 4½ *maravedís*.

1660   Antonio Enríquez y Gómez, *Academias morales*, Madrid. 4 *maravedís*.

1692   *Justa literaria, certamen poético o sagrado influxo en la solemne . . . canonización de . . . San Juan de Dios*, Madrid. 8 *maravedís*.

31. See *Reflexiones sobre el buen gusto en las ciencias y en las artes. traducción libre de . . . Muratori, con un discurso sobre el gusto actual de los españoles en la literatura por Don Juan Sempere y Guarinos* (Madrid, 1782), pp. 202-5.

32. See A. Rodríguez-Moñino, *Historia de los catálogos de librería españoles*, p. 96.

33. ibid., pp. 92 *et seq*.

34. See Pedro Gómez Aparicio, *Historia del Periodismo español desde la 'Gaceta de Madrid' (1661) hasta el destronamiento de Isabel II* (Madrid, 1967).

35. F. M. Nipho, *Viaje de la razón por la Europa por el marqués Caracciolo*, Parte Segunda, ed. consulted (Madrid, 1799), f 4 v. ('En la segunda Impresión de este Viage de la Razón he puesto de cursiva todas las sentencias . . . porque no se malogren en ciertos lectores, que leen de prisa, y por mera curiosidad, y tienen poco menos que muerta la reflexión'.)

36. The 'Carta de un *quidam*, a un amigo suyo, en que le describe el rosario de los cómicos de esta corte' first appeared in the *Diario de Madrid*,

No. 226, 13 de agosto de 1788. Professor E. F. Helman has published a hitherto unknown satirical poem of Jovellanos first printed in 1797 in the same periodical (see *PSA* 157, 9-30).

37. A trivial sonnet by Meléndez to Gregorio de Salas was printed in the *Correo de Madrid*, No. 205, 8 de noviembre de 1788. This and other poems published by Meléndez in periodicals are listed in Georges Demerson, *Don Juan Meléndez Valdés et son temps* (Paris, 1962), pp. 614-15.

38. See *Obras de Don Juan Pablo Forner*, recogidas y ordenadas por Don Luis Villanueva (Madrid, 1844), p. [xxiv], 'Catálogo de mis obras'.

39. I recently bought from a Madrid bookseller *La estafeta del Placer. Continuación de las obras de Don Lucas Alemán y Aguado. Tomo LXXXIIII*. The manuscript volume consists entirely of short pieces, 'unas jocosas y otras serias', such as Alemán published in the *Correo de Madrid*.

40. Quevedo, *España defendida y los tiempos de ahora, de las calumnias de los noveleros y sediciosos*, ed. with an introduction and notes by R. Selden Rose (Madrid, 1916), pp. 7-10, 22-6, 67-71.

41. ibid., ed. René Radouart (Paris, 1920), p. 46.

42. See Montesquieu's *Lettres persanes*, *Lettre LXXVIII*; Saint-Evremond's views are summarised in Ramón Esquerra's article 'Juicios de Saint-Evremond sobre España', *BH*, XXXVIII (1936), 353-63.

43. See Juan Francisco de Masdeu, *Historia crítica de España y de la cultura española* (Madrid, 1783-1805), I, 177.

44. See Serrano y Sanz, 'El Consejo de Castilla y la censura de libros en el siglo XVIII', *RABM*, XV (1906), 45-6.

45. See his prologue to *La literatura española demostrada por el erudito Don Nicolas Antonio* (Madrid, 1787). Another defence to appear the same year was Valladares y Sotomayor's *Prospecto* for the first volume of his *Semanario erudito*, pp. 1-3.

46. See his 'Oración en alabanza de las obras de Don Diego Saavedra Fajardo', in *Ensayos oratorios* (Madrid, 1739), pp. 129, 141-2.

47. Ignacio de Luzán, *La Poética*, con un estudio de Luigi de Filippo (Barcelona, 1956), I, 33.

48. See his *Discurso II sobre las Tragedias españolas* (Madrid, 1753), pp. 4-5.

49. In the prologue to his *Colección de pensamientos filosóficos, sentencias, y dichos grandes de los más célebres poetas dramáticos españoles formada por el corresponsal del Censor* (Madrid, 1786), I.

50. See N. Glendinning, 'La fortuna de Góngora en el siglo XVIII', *RFE*, XIV, 1961 (1963), 345-6.

51. See Russell P. Sebold, 'A Statistical Analysis of the Origins and Nature of Luzán's Ideas on Poetry', *HR*, XXXV (1967), 227-51.

52. See N. Glendinning, 'Influencia de la literatura inglesa en España en el siglo XVIII', 69 (note 63) and 91-2 (note 119).

53. See *Certamen literario en el qual el Seminario de Nobles de San Ignacio de la Compañía de Jesús* . . . (Valencia, 1764), p. 3; and *Examen general del Real Seminario de Nobles. Año de 1829* (Madrid, 1829), *passim*.

54. *Exercicios públicos de historia literaria que tendrán en los Estudios Reales de Madrid* · . . *en* . . . *septiembre de 1790* (Madrid, n.d.), f A 4 r.

55. A study of the various impressions of this work is badly needed. I have seen at least one set in which Vol. III had a title-page with the date 1782 (instead of 1770 or 1773), and Vol. VII also had 1782 (instead of 1773).

56. See Cadalso's *Quintillas de estilo y conceptos antiguos sobre yerros amorosos* and Moratín's *Canción en lenguage antiguo, y en el metro de Juan de Mena,* en elogio del Infante Don Gabriel, dirigida al rey, con motivo de la traducción de Salustio hecha por S.A. (in *Poesías inéditas de D. Nicolás Fernández de Moratín,* publicadas por R. Foulché Delbosc (Madrid, 1892), pp. 7-9).

57. See Isidoro Montiel, 'Dos traductores de Ossian en España: Alonso Ortiz y el ex-jesuita Montengón', *RN,* IX (1967), 77–84.

58. See Nigel Glendinning, 'Influencia de la literatura inglesa en España en el siglo XVIII', 91–2, note 119.

59. Félix de Abreu maintained that Spaniards read the works of Voltaire and Rousseau despite the fact, or indeed because of the fact, that they were forbidden (see Joseph Baretti, *A Journey from London to Genoa, through England, Portugal, Spain and France,* 3rd ed. (London, 1770), II, 318–19). Cadalso's laudatory references to Voltaire tend to be oblique in print, however, or omitted by the censors or editors altogether in the 1770s and 1780s (see *Los eruditos a la violeta,* ed. N. Glendinning, Salamanca–Madrid–Barcelona–Caracas, 1968, pp. 51, 66, 68, 69, and 70; and the *Cartas marruecas,* ed. L. Dupuis and N. Glendinning (London, 1966), p. 112). Fray Pedro Rodríguez Morzo announced his translation of the *Oráculo de los nuevos filósofos, M. Voltaire impugnado por sus mismas obras con la refutación de la obra de Emilio de Juan Jacobo Rousseau* in the *Gaceta de Madrid* for 19 June 1770. But a number of Voltaire's plays were translated for the *Reales Sitios* that year, and a translation of the *Micromégas* was published without mention of the author's name by Blas Corchos in Madrid in 1786.

60. See Jefferson Rea Spell, *Rousseau in the Spanish World before 1833. A study in Franco-Spanish literary Relations* (Austin, 1938).

61. Leandro Fernández de Moratín, Letter to Forner dated Montpellier, 23 March 1787, *Obras póstumas de Moratín,* II (Madrid, 1867), 78.

62. See Á. González Palencia, 'Meléndez Valdés y la literatura de cordel', *Entre dos siglos* (Madrid, 1943), especially p. 207; see also Julio Caro Baroja, *Ensayo sobre la literatura de cordel* (Madrid, Revista de Occidente, 1968), especially chapter 17.

63. Speaking of the second half of the eighteenth century, Agustín Durán maintained that 'apenas entonces teníamos un crítico que osase defender nuestra antigua literatura considerándola en sí misma, y como medio para recuperar la perdida originalidad e independencia que debiera nacer de la unión de lo pasado con lo presente' (see *BAE,* 10, p. vi). Durán himself, who was familiar with Schlegel's theories, saw the ballads and the theatre of the Golden Age as a reflection of the Spanish national character Others express similar views at much the same period—from the 1820s onwards more particularly.

Chapter 2

EIGHTEENTH-CENTURY PROSE

THE OLD DIVISION OF STYLES into 'high', 'middle', and 'low', each appropriate for particular subjects and effects, persisted in eighteenth-century literary theory. Style was still a means to an end and not an end in itself; less a reflection of the man who was writing, than of the subject he was writing about. The eighteenth-century author expected to have to write in different ways in different works. Leandro Fernández de Moratín used the mock heroic or sublime for his satire on pedantry *La derrota de los pedantes*, and 'middle' for his *Apuntaciones sueltas de Inglaterra*, which describe with wit and understatement the manners and customs he found in England in the 1790s. Style could also be 'wrong' in eighteenth-century terms. It was a mistake according to Cadalso for his friends Moratín and Iglesias to use the sublime style for obviously unsublime subjects like fellow-poets and Inquisitors-General.

Other terms than 'high', 'middle', and 'low' applied to style are basically variants on these and in no way different in concept. The geographical styles commonly referred to by Cicero and other Classical theorists were still current—Laconic, Attic, Rhodian, and Asiatic. The last of these was the opposite of the more familiar first, and stood for variety of words and expressions, pomposity, and resonance; Attic and Rhodian were less extreme and more generally favoured by Spanish theorists, particularly in the second half of the century. At that period excessive decoration was roundly condemned: the abuse of sententiousness, tropes, word-play and puns, antitheses and so forth, thought to be characteristic of Gracián and Quevedo.

In the first few decades of the eighteenth century, however, Gracián and Quevedo were still the commonest models for Spanish prose. Their influence is partly reflected by, and partly no doubt the result of, the considerable number of editions of their works available at that time. The decline in editions of Gracián in the course of the century obviously echoes the changing taste of the period (see below, Appendix c).

Quevedo in particular provided early eighteenth-century writers with forms and structures as well as examples of successful rhetorical techniques. The short satirical work *Virtud al uso y mística a la moda* (1729) by 'Fulgencio Afán de Ribera' is a case in point, and its style has led some critics to assume that it belongs to the seventeenth century.[1] *Virtud al uso*, obviously cast in the same mock-pedagogical style as the section 'Para saber todas las ciencias y artes mecánicas y liberales en un día' of Quevedo's *Libro de todas las cosas*, consists of letters from an older man (Don Alejandro Girón) to his son, 'el Hermano Carlos de el Niño Jesús', enclosing a series of documents with advice on modes of conduct and dress to convince the general public of his piety; the whole constituting a series of picaresque lessons in the gentle art of hypocrisy. Other aspects of the work—the letter-form, and the fiction-within-a-fiction device (according to the prologue the work was a manuscript found in a bed and picked up, along with some fleas, by the publisher)—also follow seventeenth-century Spanish precedents, like Quevedo's *Epístolas del Caballero de la Tenaza* and *Don Quixote*.

The impact of Quevedo's style and ideas makes itself still more strongly felt in imitations of the *Sueños*. Torres Villarroel's (1693-1770) *Sueños morales* (1727 and 1728) is an early instance, and the tradition continues later in the century in works like Ramírez de Góngora's *Óptica del Cortejo* (Córdoba, 1774), which criticises the immorality of *cortejos* (male companions or lovers) in the form of a dream about the Palace of Love, in which 'el entendimiento' shows the narrator a series of scenes in a sort of magic-lantern show, much as Desengaño conducts Quevedo on a moral tour of life in *El mundo por de dentro*. Later still, short *sueños morales* found their way into the pages of the *Correo de Madrid* (1787-90), and the dream form was adapted to literary criticism in the anonymous *El no se opone de muchos y residencia de ingenios, su autor, D.M.D.Q.B.* (Madrid, 1789).

Torres's *Sueños* was the most widely read and reprinted of these works in Spain, and the central fiction of the dream and the idea of a guided tour of existence clearly come from *El mundo por de dentro*. In Torres's work, however, it is the author himself who guides, and his companion—the shade of Quevedo—who asks the questions; and while Quevedo's Desengaño leads him through allegorical streets, Torres walks the real streets of the Spanish capital. The Madrid environment at first sight appears to limit the moral scope of Torres's work, though it roots it more firmly in reality; but many of the specific professions satirised lead to general points of morality much as they did in Quevedo. Real differences of approach begin to emerge when one takes a look at the underlying structures. The walk through Madrid streets gives Torres's work a superficially coherent pattern: the logic which takes him from 'los letrados' to 'Químicos y médicos' is the logic which takes him from the Casa de los Consejos to the Plazuela de Palacio—a short walk down the Calle Mayor.[2] The logic of Quevedo's Sueños, on the other hand, is rather more subtle: it leads the reader from the surface appearance of one group in society to its underlying moral nature, and then on, in a repeating pattern, to another group. It does not matter whether the group is a 'real' one like the tailors or soldiers, or a 'moral' one like the 'I thought thats' or 'I wish I hads', the underlying logic is the same, and Quevedo is able to preserve a sense of unity while moving from one group to another since all are equally morally corrupt. Torres, in fact, seems prepared to sacrifice unifying structure for the sake of variety, and he shifts from the immoral or useless to the moral or useful as they strike his eye. In Torres, therefore, we pass from the Jesuit Seminary in the Calle de Toledo, which is praised, to the old clothes-merchants in the Plazuela de la Cebada, just off the same street, who are condemned.[3]

Further differences between Torres and Quevedo are observable at the level of sentence structure. Both writers, for example, make a good deal of use of wit, word-play, and metaphorical language, but the ways in which they use this material are not the same. If we compare apparently similar descriptions, differences soon leap to the eye. Take a passage from Quevedo's description of the Licenciado Cabra, for example:

> . . . los ojos avecindados en el cogote, que parece miraba por cuévanos; tan hundidos y escuros, que era buen sitio el suyo para tienda de mercaderes: la nariz ertre Roma y Francia, porque se le había comido de unas bubas de resfriado; que aun no fueron del vicio, porque cuestan dinero: las barbas descoloridas de miedo de

la boca vecina, que, de pura hambre parece que amenaza a comérselas . . .[4]

We can follow this with a Quevedesque description from Torres of an equally lean and hungry individual:

Era el buen fantasma un ayuno con sombrero, una dieta con pies, un desmayo con barbas y una carencia con calzones. Unas veces parecía el cuello bajón y otras calabaza; tan hundido de ojos que juzgué que miraba por bucina; cada respiración traía a las ancas dos bostezos. Todo era indicio de estómago en pena, de tripas en vacante y de hambreón descomunal.[5]

The differences here are perhaps reflected in the punctuation. Quevedo flows in a stream; Torres falls in a light patter. Above all, Quevedo's description is a unity in a variety of ways. In the first place, it is held together by an extended travel metaphor: 'ojos avecindados', 'buen sitio', 'entre Roma y Francia', 'la boca vecina'. Secondly, the visual parallels are not just ends in themselves, but are used to make intellectual, moral points about the character of the person described. The inadequate diet of Cabra is a reflection of his meanness and hypocrisy as well as a thing in itself: the hollows of his eyes conjure up the dark corners in which merchants conduct their crooked deals; the sores on his nose are not venereal, because he is too mean to be vicious. Even the images which appear at first sight to be purely visual turn out to be related to the rest of the description on closer scrutiny. Thus the image of the eyes which look out through grape baskets not only fits visually—the stained wicker-work being singularly appropriate to inflamed hollows or red lids— but also relates to the other food and drink images (or rather, lack-of-food-and-drink images) which are meaningfully used throughout the passage. Torres, on the other hand, gets carried away by his decorative, repetitive patterns ('dieta/desmayo'; 'carencia/calzones'); and he is often content with sound effects, visual parallels, and piece-meal imagery, appealing in fact to the Fancy, in Coleridge's terms, rather than the Imagination. His parallels may add sonority or pro-vide pleasing grotesques for the mind's eye to contemplate, but they do not always add to the meaning of the whole.[6] Neither of the two comparisons Torres uses for the neck in the description, for instance —the bassoon and the marrow—contributes more than a lively visual point, and the images summoned up by 'bucina', 'traer a las ancas', and the soul in torment implied in 'estómago en pena' have no special relevance in the context.

This approach of Torres to imagery is not uncharacteristic. Even when he attempts an extended metaphor, as he does in the 'Preámbulo al sueño' at the beginning of the *Primeras visitas de Torres y Quevedo por Madrid,* the author's fancy and fascination with words merely lead him into byways and away from the highroads of his subject.[7] Indeed, his preference for playing with words rather than with ideas marks an essential difference between his writing and that of Quevedo. The latter uses much word-play in his *Cuento de cuentos,* but this is in order to mock the slang expressions which debase the Spanish language in his view. Torres, on the other hand, in his imitation of this work of Quevedo, called *Historia de las historias* (1736), has a more ambiguous approach. His overt intention is to represent 'some of the illegitimacy and adultery of our ways of speaking', and yet his delight in these expressions which give 'variety' and 'richness' to the Spanish language is also apparent.[8]

Torres, however, should not be written off as a pale reflection of a seventeenth-century master and essentially unserious. He was conscious of having a mixed nature,[9] and there is perhaps a deeper dichotomy in his work between the serious and the frivolous than there was in Quevedo. His imitations of Quevedo in fact extend to the serious side, and he wrote variations on the latter's *Los remedios de cualquier fortuna* entitled *Las recetas de Torres añadidas a los remedios de cualquier fortuna,* as well as works in a deep moralistic vein such as the *Cátedra de morir* and two lives of religious figures. Some idea of the balance between seriousness and farce in his work can perhaps be gained from his own *Vida*—a balance represented emblematically on the title-page of the Madrid 1743 edition by the cherub holding a mirror on the right, another holding a cross on the left, and symbols of Jesus and the Virgin Mary, which fill the space between. At the same time the balance can often be a reflection of the Horatian doctrine of 'teaching and delighting' rather than of the character of Torres himself, as it clearly is, for instance, in some of his scientific work.

In content as well as in form, Torres's work continues earlier traditions. If some of his scientific conservatism can be attributed to fear of the Inquisition, his apparently up-to-date interest in experi-

mental science is really only a reflection of his reverence for Bacon.
His respect for traditional social and religious hierarchies is also
unswerving—another contrast between Torres and Quevedo. He
appears almost naïvely proud of his contacts with the nobility,
although he is willing to write down to the more common people.
In the Third Part of his *Vida* he openly expresses his gladness that
his daring has not plunged him into 'the miserable depths of unbelief,
ignorance of God's precepts, of the royal ordinances, and the established order of society and nature'.[10] It is hardly surprising that the
picaresque aspects of his life—like the style in which he wrote about
them—provided lessons in conformism rather than serious chal-
lenges to hierarchies, and that the first subscribers to his complete
works in 1752 were solidly 'establishment'.[11]

Torres's works reflect a common pattern of modified but basically
traditional styles and attitudes. Other contemporaries, however,
clearly favour change. Padre Feijoo (1676-1764), by comparison
with Torres, seems almost a revolutionary spirit, and certainly his
contribution to changes in Spain was widely recognised in the
eighteenth century. Admittedly he was backed in the publication of
his works by the Benedictine Order and by the king, and he
dedicated his writings in the main to princes and prelates. Yet the
respect he expressed for inherited nobility at the beginning of his
Honra y provecho de la agricultura extended to the title only and not
necessarily to the person who held it, and he was more deeply com-
mitted to the experimental sciences than was Torres. Experimental
physics he declared to be the only useful science, and was almost
apologetic when he could not check a theory for himself by experimentation.[12] He respected the conclusions reached by such scientists
as Homberg, Réaumur, Boyle, Newton, and others, and even
encouraged his readers to experiment for themselves with simple
objects like coins and saucepans.[13] At the same time he avoided
denigrating more traditional approaches to science, and could
describe himself as 'neither a slave to Aristotle nor an ally of his
enemies'.[14]

An essential difference between Torres and Feijoo lies in their
awareness of work being done in the rest of Europe. Torres had
been to Portugal, but otherwise had very little contact with foreign
countries or the publications on scientific topics they produced.
Feijoo, on the other hand, who rarely left Oviedo, read the pro-

ceedings of European scientific societies and academies, the *Mémoires de Trévoux* and *Journal des Savants,* and endeavoured to keep up with current scientific theory. He was quick to take an interest in new ideas and, indeed, mistakenly based his own theory about the cause of the Lisbon earthquake on the recently discovered phenomena of electricity in the 1750s. He was also less prejudiced about foreign ideas in general, although he did not hesitate to defend Spain against some foreign criticisms in his *Glorias de España.*

In style as well as in his approach to his subjects Feijoo often broke away from the seventeenth-century traditions many of his contemporaries still admired and imitated. He disapproved of the elaborate and decorated manner of writing which was typical of the previous generation and criticised his contemporaries when they adopted it. He attacks one work for its 'impropio y afectado estilo',[15] and in the *Paralelo de las lenguas castellana y francesa* he inveighs equally rhetorically against

> una afectación pueril de tropos retóricos, por la mayor parte vulgares; una multitud de epítetos sinónimos, una colocación violenta de voces pomposas que hacen el estilo, no gloriosamente majestuoso, sí asquerosamente entumecido.[16]

Proper sublimity and magnificence he distinguishes from this 'estilo hinchado', and he prefers naturalness and spontaneity. Artifice itself should be natural and not forced, and he admires the style of Mlle de Scudéry and Fontenelle precisely because they achieve beauty in a natural way. For Feijoo their works are like 'gardens in which the flowers spring forth spontaneously rather than canvases on which they are carefully painted'.[17]

In his own works Feijoo puts these precepts into practice. In an important passage on his own style in his prologue to the second volume of the *Teatro crítico universal* he speaks of the proper use of the three styles, high, middle, and low, 'consignando a la moción de afectos el sublime, a la instrucción el mediano y a la chanza el humilde'. At the same time he is prepared to disregard the rules when nature encourages him to do so: 'Todo me dejo a la naturalidad', he affirms.

> Si en una u otra parte hallares algo del sublime, sabe que sin buscarle se me viene, o porque la calidad de la materia natural-

mente me arrebata a locuciones abigarradas, que son más eficaces cuando se trata de mover algún afecto, o porque tal vez la imaginación, por estar más caliente, me socorre de expresiones más enérgicas.[18]

This near negligence, as Feijoo himself calls it, is more apparent than real. He is perfectly prepared to use stylistic tricks if they are not too complicated or pretentious, and there is no lack of artifice in his work. He varies the topics within each volume of his *Teatro crítico* to increase their digestibility, and is not above bringing in anecdotes 'to entertain the reader with something diverting',[19] even when not strictly relevant. He also has recourse to fictional devices from time to time (though none as extravagant as those of Torres); the article *Balanza de Astrea* takes the form of an imaginary letter from an old lawyer to his young son 'recently called to the bar'. Similarly there is considerable skill in the way in which he builds up rhetorical climaxes to drive home his points with repeated grammatical structures, or to emphasise his arguments emotionally with a series of metaphors, balancing phrases, or rhetorical questions and exclamations:

> ¿Cuántas borracheras, cuántos desórdenes de gula y de lujuria, cuántas pendencias, cuántos homicidios ocasiona la abundancia de vino, que evitaría su escasez? Pero faltando el pan, ¡ay, Dios!, ¡qué triste, qué funesto, qué horrible teatro es todo un reino! Todo es lamentos, todo es ayes, todo gemidos.[20]

The structure of his essays also reflects his feeling for restraint. Generally there is a simple logical pattern with few digressions. His *Antipatía de franceses y españoles,* for instance, opens with general observations about the causes of concord and discord, and then goes on to consider the particular case of the antipathy between France and Spain. Taking two theories about the antipathy in turn, Feijoo brings evidence to discredit both, and then, in Section 2, he follows up the view that the antipathy between French and Austrians had spread to Spain, via Austrian domination, with a briefer passage on the possibility that antipathy is due to differences of character (and a digression on the question as to whether love follows more easily when people are alike or unlike). Section 3 illustrates a further way in which discord between nations can arise, and shows how small differences in constitution or circumstances led to trouble between the Turks and the Persians. And the final section proves that the antipathy between French and Spanish is not deep-rooted by citing the harmonious relations between the two peoples at the time Feijoo is writing.

The structure in fact follows the process of weighing evidence and evaluating theories with which Feijoo is concerned in all his essays. Lack of proper analysis leads to the ill-founded beliefs that Feijoo is trying to shake: 'considero indispensablemente obligados los escritores a batallar por la verdad y purgar al pueblo de su error'.[21] But this analytical process sometimes leads Feijoo back into the syllogistic argumentation which he considered outdated in Spanish universities.[22] His inbred respect for authority also makes him less critical of religious, historical, and especially of Classical, material than one would expect. If the essays are arguments they are rather one-voiced and often even one-sided. Feijoo, in fact, only makes minor modifications within the general framework of the religious beliefs and the hierarchical society he accepts. Thus, although he shares with Fontenelle a desire to enlighten and to spread a knowledge of science, he lacks the French writer's ability to think and write in terms of dialogue, and some of his complacent acceptance of aristocratic values is almost nauseating to the modern reader.

A similar position to Feijoo's is that of Padre Isla (1703-81). He too was critical of some seventeenth-century styles and traditions persisting in Spain, and was conscious of foreign criticism, though cautious in his acceptance of new theories. His style shows the same kind of basic restraint as Feijoo, and his first important work, the *Triunfo del amor y de la lealtad. Día grande de Navarra* (1746), rejects the high-flown style and artificial manner of writing. Style and narrative in fact combine in that work to deflate hollow pomp and circumstance. Wit and word-play, though very much in the Quevedan tradition, are not as exaggerated as they are in Torres, and Isla keeps closer to normal reality than Quevedo in his grotesques.

A description of nightfall gives a fair idea of Isla's early satirical style:

> Llegó la Noche; pero eso quisiera ella: iba a entrarse muy de rebozo en Pamplona, para tener parte en la fiesta; mas fue conocida, y ain permitir que descubriese la cara, se quedó a buenas

noches, porque la hicieron ir más que de paso a otra parte. El caso fue, que aquella tarde no hubo tiempo entre dos luces, sino entre muchas. . . .

In Padre Isla's novel *Fray Gerundio de Campazas* (Part I, 1758; Part II, 1770), the ridicule is sharper and the target more controversial. If the satire of the *Día grande* had merely upset the ruling classes in Pamplona, the attack on preachers in *Fray Gerundio* disturbed members of religious orders all over Spain. Furthermore, Isla's novel not only mocked the high-flown *conceptista* style affected by some religious, but extended its attack to certain scientific developments, more particularly those associated with experimental methods. Traditionalists resented the mocking of monks, while the enlightened disliked the comments on modern science.

Stylistically, most of the roots of Isla's novel lie in the seventeenth century, although the criticism of an inflated metaphorical style reflects the Classical eighteenth-century leanings of its author. The protagonist—a particular case illustrating the general way in which a false view of oratory can warp a weak personality—is clearly in the tradition of *Don Quixote*. Yet *Fray Gerundio* is also close to the traditions of comedy in which the audience laughs at a misshapen character without identifying with him, and there are echoes of Molière in Isla's work as well as of Cervantes.[23]

The most obvious debt to *Don Quixote* is the supposition that *Fray Gerundio* is a manuscript written up by Isaac Ibrahim Abusemblat, suffragan bishop of Cairo, and the protagonist's head is turned by reading Baroque sermons as Don Quixote's was by reading the novels of chivalry. But the structure of Isla's novel is really much simpler than that of Cervantes, and the didactic purposes much more explicit. The major 'disparates' of Fray Gerundio are followed by solid correctives which show what he should have done. The ex-provincial, the *beneficiado*, and Maestro Prudencio in Books II and III; the *Apuntamientos sobre los vicios del estilo* and the Magistral in Book IV; the Familiar and the Benedictine abbot in Book V, constantly point to the mistakes of Fray Gerundio and suggest the proper course of action for him to adopt. If there is some variety on the irrational side—Fray Blas to share and encourage Gerundio's false stylistic and moral standards and numerous lesser figures like the village priest in Pero Rucio who fail to see through their elaborate and ridiculous façade—the voice of reason is loud, and only the skill of Isla as a writer, his wit and perceptiveness in matters of human behaviour, save the work from being unreadable today. Fortunately there is a good deal of linguistic vitality in the work. There has to be, since the action of the novel is minimal. At one extreme Isla gives us the pompous pseudo-poetic outpourings and ridiculous logic of Fray Gerundio's sermons; at the other, the dialect conversations of characters like 'el familiar' (a *gracioso* figure straight out of the Spanish *comedia*); and in between a wide range of other middle and low styles—irony from characters like the Benedictine abbot, chatty intellectual conversation between monks, exaggerated gallicisms from the pretentious, and racier low-style exchanges from humbler characters.

All these linguistic patterns help the verisimilitude of the work in its various episodes. But the range of reality covered is limited—intentionally so—to fit the theme. Around the central topic of sermon-style are grouped related topics like the education of the friar (both as child and as novice) and education in general; religious morality; and the problem of ignorance and false values in all classes of society. Isla advocates reason and order on all these fronts. The good sermon can influence and educate the society which listens to it, since those of humble birth are as capable of following rational discourse as the nobility. A high-flown, irrational sermon, on the other hand, encourages ignorance and a false sense of values, attention to exteriors—verbiage, dress, and gesture—rather than the mind or the soul.

Ultimately, then, Padre Isla's novel has an important part to play in the mid-century reform movement in social as well as stylistic matters. The fact that it links the reform of style to the reform of morality is typical of Spanish Neo-classicism. Equally characteristic is Isla's concern to relate literature as closely as possible to the reality of his times,[24] although it was in some ways too close for comfort—since some of Isla's characters were recognisable to his contemporaries and the Second Part could not be published. The denial of the novel's supposed documentary character at the end of the final part is supremely ironic.

So far Spanish writers had been largely content to create works within existing Spanish styles and traditions. But increasing contact with the rest of Europe and the growing awareness of French,

English, and Italian literature, referred to in Chapter I, now led to an exploration of international forms, some of them new to Spain.

In prose, one of the first to adopt an obviously European style was José Clavijo y Fajardo (1730-1806), whose periodical *El Pensador* began to appear weekly in 1762. The model for this was clearly Addison's *Spectator*. Seven whole Speculations are translated and there are direct imitations of at least six others.[25] From Addison, Clavijo y Fajardo takes the apparently personal view of society, the variety of subjects (sometimes specific and social, at others more general and philosophical), and the fondness for making generalisations. He also adopts Addison's technique of incorporating fictional letters from imaginary people (sometimes of exotic Oriental origin) into his weekly articles, and apparently eavesdrops on *tertulias* as Addison seemingly sits in on London coffee-house conversations. Some of Clavijo's fictional devices, however, have sources in Spanish XII); superstition (*Pensamiento* XXXV); even bull-fights (*Pensamientos* XLVII and XLIX) seems to look back to Quevedo's *La hora de todos y la Fortuna con seso* as well as abroad to Fénelon and Fontenelle's *Dialogues des morts*.

So far as the topics themselves are concerned, Clavijo gives voice to many of the questions which preoccupied enlightened Spaniards at the time: education, for instance (*Pensamientos* II, VIII, and XII); superstition (*Pensamiento* XXXV); even bull-fights (*Pensamientos* XLVIII and LI). As he writes in *Pensamiento* II, his intention is that his essays 'llevarán casi siempre un espíritu de reforma'. On the reform of literature he is ironic in his defence of the disorganised nature of the seventeenth-century Spanish theatre in *Pensamiento* III, and openly favours Classical and moralising forms of drama in *Pensamientos* IX, XXII, XXIII, XXVI, and XXVII. He looks to Luzán's *Poética* and seventeenth-century Classicists like José Antonio González de Salas for satisfactory definitions and precepts;[26] praises Isla for his stand on the style of sermons;[27] and mocks or criticises hyperbolic and exaggeratedly metaphoric language in *Pensamientos* XXX and LIV. In his approach to society he seems less openly a reforming spirit. His avoidance of matters of government in the discussion of plans for his periodical in *Pensamiento* I might be attributed to fear of the censorship, but he clearly accepts the hierarchical nature of Spanish society without hesitation in *Pensamiento* XV as necessary 'para mantener el orden en la sociedad'.

No estoy mal con las jerarquías que forman la desigualdad de condiciones, y que en nuestro estado son precisas para mantener el orden en la sociedad. Más. Me alegro de las distinciones que gozan los Príncipes, los Grandes, y los señores y personas de mérito. Si algunas veces se ve en ellas un número distintivo, debido sólo al nacimiento, también se suele ver una pequeña parte del premio que merece la virtud.

Like Feijoo, however, Clavijo clearly has no respect for un-virtuous, unjust, or unuseful princes or nobles. This begins to emerge in *Pensamiento* xv ('Del ceremonial de tratamientos') where Clavijo shows how the traditional submissiveness of people towards those higher up the social scale can lead to a kind of tyranny. Still stronger points are made in the following *Pensamiento* xvi ('De la crítica sobre las leyes en general'), where the basic concept is evidently that of Rousseau's social pact and the need for the people to be familiar with the laws that protect their rights and interests. Looking back over the history of Rome Clavijo shows how many tyrants have managed to avoid the rule of law in the past: 'Para un Tito, ¡cuántos Nerones!', he exclaims,

> Para un Marco Aurelio, ¡cuántos Calígulas! . . . ¡ Qué corto es el número de los poderosos, a quienes la ley ha servido de freno! ¡Y qué inmenso el de aquellos, que no han conocido más ley que la de su capricho!

In fact Clavijo reveals here and elsewhere his fundamental concern for social justice. His preoccupations are with society as a whole, not merely with the establishment, and with the way in which the virtues and vices of individuals affect the lives of others. Obviously, given the existence of the censorship, Clavijo could not, even if he had wanted to, query the whole organisation of the Spanish state. But he goes as far as he can in arguing for equality, even if, for example, his concern for a fairer distribution of wealth finds its only possible outlet in a passionate recommendation that those with money should give to those who lack it, rather than waste their wealth on the pointless pomp of marriage feasts or similar exercises.[28]

Clavijo's *Pensador*, in fact, is one of the first eighteenth-century Spanish works which sets out to provoke discussion and debate. Its form was probably designed to reach a wide public, and certainly allowed the examination of topics from more than one point of view. Even within *Pensamientos*, Clavijo often asks questions and seeks alternative answers, and *Pensamiento* XXXIV, 'Crítica de varios legisladores y filósofos y contra algunas necedades humanas', is a fine example of the effectiveness of his method.

Pensamiento XXXIV begins with a mocking exposé of the legal theories of some of the great figures of Classical antiquity. It goes on to criticise the exaggerated confidence in their systems shown by a number of ancient and modern philosophers (Aristotle, Descartes, Newton, and Gassendi) and to praise the more tentative approaches of Locke and his followers. An attack on Schools and Universities ensues (for their lack of utility), and there is another on fashions, which are not in the interest of society as a whole. This leads on to a criticism of philosophers—perhaps Clavijo has Feijoo in mind— who, 'por un vano amor proprio, y deseo de ostentar luces superiores a los comunes se ponen a desengañar a los hombres de errores útiles a los mismos hombres'. (Illusions which are useful, like posthumous fame, should not be shaken; prejudices may serve as stimuli.)[29] And the essay ends with the philosopher's lament over the impossibility of putting things right, and his need for a friend with whom he can communicate.

The whole of this *Pensamiento* is a somewhat pessimistic analysis of the philosopher's role: first fated to be wrong, then right but unhelpful, and finally anxious to be helpful but powerless to be so. And yet even 'analysis' is an overstatement as a description of the essay. It purports to be a letter to Clavijo from some unknown correspondent; so we do not really know what Clavijo himself 'officially' thinks about these matters at the end of it. What better way of forcing the reader to reflect on the subject under discussion, as Clavijo's 'correspondent' does, for himself?

Clavijo's interests in individual feelings and above all in European styles were soon taken a good deal further by the group of writers who met regularly in the Fonda de San Sebastián in Madrid in the early 1770s. Unlike earlier known literary *tertulias*, this one was international in its very nature and included a number of Italian as well as Spanish writers. Napoli Signorelli, an authority on the European theatre, as well as Nicolás Fernández de Moratín, Tomás de Iriarte, José Cadalso, and Ignacio López de Ayala, attended its meetings. French and Italian poetry was read and discussed as well as works by contemporary Spanish writers.

As a prosewriter Cadalso (1741-82) is clearly the most original member of the group. He begins in a solidly Spanish and Classical tradition with poems in the manner of Garcilaso and Villegas, and his first published prose work—the satire *Los eruditos a la violeta* (1772)—followed the *Virtud al uso* in borrowing forms and humorous techniques from Quevedo's *Libro de todas las cosas*. But the subject of *Los eruditos* is directly related to the debate in Spain about international ideas and styles, and in it, as in his other works, Cadalso tried to keep a balance between nationalism and internationalism, tradition and change, in form and content.

Both his *Noches lúgubres* and the *Cartas marruecas* have formal and ideological roots in foreign literature,[30] and both take Clavijo's concern for discussion and debate much further than the author of *El Pensador*. The *Noches lúgubres* is in dialogue form for a start, and the possibilities of variety are increased by the radically different class background of the two main characters, Tediato and Lorenzo; the former 'nacido en cuna más delicada', the latter a poor grave-digger. The topics they discuss introduce some of the major topics of the Enlightenment: the nature of fortune and the nature of man; reason and unreason; whether there is a benevolent force at work in the universe; whether anything deserves respect or love; the nature of justice; the desirability of suicide. The plot itself is thought-provoking, since it involves the paradox of the rational man, Tediato, contemplating and putting into effect an irrational act by digging up the body of his dead mistress, and seeking death when he is wrong-fully imprisoned. These topics, the nocturnal setting, and also the poetic prose in which much of the work is written, together with more traditional fictional techniques like character contrast and suspense, combined to make the work appeal powerfully to Cadalso's contemporaries and readers of all classes in the nineteenth century.[31] The qualified pessimism Cadalso expressed about life and the universe, and the sympathetic treatment of doubt and the irrational, made it a dangerous work in its own time and a victim of the Inquisition in the early nineteenth century.[32]

Equally advanced in its discussion of many Enlightenment topics was Cadalso's *Cartas marruecas*, which accepts the morality of the Moors and their religious beliefs as readily as those of the Christians in the central characters (the two Moors Ben-Beley and Gazel, and the Christian Nuño,[33] whose name perhaps echoes that of the ninth-century count Nuño Núñez who aided the Asturian king against the Moors at the battle of Pancorbo, exemplifying the traditional Spanish patriot.) It criticises abuse of social status by politicians who favour their relatives, and aristocrats or magnates who are not useful to society (*Cartas* LI and LXIII), and implies that rulers who do not have a proper care for the interests of their people are blameworthy (*Carta* III). While Cadalso praises the Bourbon kings, and respects their paternalistic concept of the monarchy (*Carta* LXXIII), he attacks the Habsburgs for sacrificing the economic wellbeing of the country to wars which only furthered their personal political ambitions (*Carta* III). The extent to which such views were difficult for a Spaniard to express openly at the period is evident from the modifications editors and censors made to these passages in their editions of Cadalso's work.[34] His unpublished *Defensa de la nación española contra la Carta persiana* LXXVIII *de Montesquieu* could afford to be more outspoken and described Philip II as 'rey perjudicial a su pueblo', and the three subsequent monarchs as 'tres descendientes suyos *a cual más inútil*'.[35]

The *Cartas marruecas* is also interesting for its relativism. Cadalso's clearest assertion of relativism occurs in his *Defensa* . . . , where he says: 'Todo es respectivo en este mundo, no hay cosa que sea positivamente tal'.[36] This idea is certainly implicit in the *Cartas marruecas* in the way in which topics are looked at from varying viewpoints in different letters. Cadalso, in fact, uses a variety of techniques to introduce different perspectives. The Moorish and Christian characters in the foreground, other Spaniards in the background, express a variety of opinions, and Gazel's travels through Spain and France introduce further diversity. The structure of the work in fact forces the reader to shift his attention from specific Spanish topics and problems to European ones and beyond that to human existence itself. An analysis of the letters reveals a very definite pattern: groups which discuss Spanish problems are interspersed with letters about general philosophical and moral questions throughout the book.[37]

This perspectivism of Cadalso, however, does not mean that the work never comes down on any particular side. On the contrary, a strong rational thread runs through the *Cartas marruecas* and the author's belief in the value of reason and discussion as a means of ascertaining what is valid and what is not, cannot be doubted. Irony and humour often point to a particular view, and individual letters may follow a train of thought or demonstrate a point with an anecdote. In *Carta* XLIII, for instance, there are in a total of nine sentences four affirmations, two humorous sentences—an ironic doubt and a comic wish—and two reinforcements of the original affirmations followed by a final mild *caveat*. The interest in the cause and effect process is as evident here as in Cadalso's *Apuntaciones autobiográficas*.[38]

The nature of the material discussed also reflects Cadalso's interest in reason, and the author's imagination is kept on a very tight rein. A high percentage of the experiences related in the *Cartas marruecas* are those of ordinary everyday life. The young Moor Gazel is obviously modelled on Al-Ghazzali, the Moorish ambassador to Madrid in the 1760s,[39] and even the dreams of the *proyectistas* in *Carta* XXXIV are close to reality. Quevedo's *proyectista* in *El Buscón* had a wild and impossible scheme for mopping up the sea with sponges;[40] Cadalso's figment of the imagination, on the other hand, merely plans to bisect the peninsula with two canals, much as had been planned in the 1750s![41]

Other mid-eighteenth-century writers also restrained their imagination. There was no Fielding or Smollett or Richardson in Spain, although the latter's work was certainly appreciated in the peninsula and imitated there before the end of the century. Even Spanish satires were more closely related to the everyday in Spain than Swift's *Gulliver's Travels* or Voltaire's *Candide*. Dictionaries are parodied for satirical ends by Luis José Velázquez[42] and, in the early nineteenth century, by Gallardo.[43] A superb lampoon on the Spanish establishment in Ferdinand VI's reign was couched in the form of a last will and testament,[44] and an attack on the distorted values of Madrid society attributed to Cadalso in 1768 took the form of a parody of the yearbook of events in the capital—the *Calendario manual*.[45] In the generation immediately after that of Cadalso and indeed in his own time too there were some attacks on individuals of a more imaginative nature—the anonymous attack on Olavide (*Vida de Don Guindo Cerezo*) and Forner's lampoon on the Iriarte family (*Los gramáticos chinos*)—but neither of these was published, and it may well have been the case that censorship as much as the

3 * *

inclination of individual writers imposed some restrictions on the imagination. For a full use of the imagination the individual perhaps needs to feel isolated from society, and while there were writers like Cadalso and Vicente García de la Huerta (1734-87) who fell out with the establishment at this period, most of them felt strong pressures to conform, since they had been born into the *hidalgo* class, and therefore into the establishment, themselves.[46]

Tomás de Iriarte's (1750-91) *Los literatos en cuaresma* (1773) seems to illustrate this point. It is a satirical work written in the form of a series of Lenten addresses devised by a *tertulia* for the good of Spanish society rather than for the good of the Christian soul. The addresses or sermons are preached by Spaniards disguised as Theophrastus, Cicero, and Cervantes and treat of unconstructive literary criticism, the education of children, and the Spanish theatre. There is a touch of religious scepticism, perhaps, in the form of the work which seems to imply that *philosophes* are as useful to society as Lenten preachers, and the work breathes the spirit of the Spanish Enlightenment in its acceptance of the need to reform the religious orders, education, and literature. But the work also reflects the common belief of Neo-classic writers that reforms were best made by an enlightened despot, or sought only through existing institutions. As Don Severo says in Iriarte's work,

> en este feliz reinado en que vivimos habréis advertido que si los arduos proyectos que ha puesto en ejecución el supremo brazo del monarca hubiesen sido emprendidos por autoridad inferior, jamás hubieran llegado a efecto, según las contradicciones con que los ha perseguido el vulgo de los críticos.[47]

As well as influencing the way in which writers expressed themselves in literature the establishment in Spain also provided some new forms in which reformist ideas could be expressed. The institutions created by the Bourbon kings or with their approval, such as the Academies and the Economic or Patriotic Societies, naturally encouraged the development of prose forms such as papers, addresses, and even poems, designed to be read at their public meetings. Jovellanos's most important ideas for reform are certainly expressed in his *Memorias* rather than in his plays or poems which seek to involve a wider public in the ideas without working them out in great detail. Open letters to politicians such as the *Cartas político-*

económicas, now attributed to Arroyal,[48] and the *Cartas sobre los obstáculos que la naturaleza, la opinión y las leyes oponen a la felicidad pública* of the conde de Cabarrús (1752-1810), reflect a similar trend. Presumably the choice between literary form or dissertation for the expression of Enlightenment ideas depended primarily on the kind of public a writer wished to reach.

Memorias and *discursos* give rise to a particularly late eighteenth-century form of prose—impassioned argumentation—which separates them from seventeenth-century theorists like Navarrete or Fernán-Núñez.[49] Jovellanos certainly goes further than Feijoo too in his use of repeated structures and pile-up sentences to arouse the emotions in the course of argument. There are notable examples in the section entitled 'Estorbos morales o derivados de la opinión' in his *Informe sobre la ley agraria,* which reaches a climax in a series of parallel questions. In contrast to the impassioned flow of his prose, however, Jovellanos's metaphors are relatively restrained. Avenues, doors, and pits are opened up; barriers erected; dykes breached. Riches (and wisdom) flow; the fortunes of agriculture are built on 'frágiles cimientos'[50] and cities are skeletons of their former selves.

More obviously intense and rhetorical than Jovellanos's *Memorias* is Forner's (1756-97) *Discurso sobre el amor de la patria* (1794), partly perhaps because it was written to be read aloud, but also because of its subject. Forner argues that patriotism holds societies together as surely as gravity the universe, and one of the climaxes of his argument is a superb piece of balanced, repeated-pattern rhetoric:

Donde reina el amor a la patria brota la felicidad de entre las manos de los hombres. Los campos florecen; las poblaciones brillan; las generaciones se multiplican; no hay campo sin cultivador; no hay familia sin patrimonio; no hay arte que se ignore, oficio que se descuide; los caminos por decirlo así hormiguean en el comercio; rebosan hacia los puertos las sobras del trabajo nacional; y trasladadas a los más remotos confines, refluyen a la patria en nueva y duplicada riqueza, que derramándose por las mismas manos que la engendraron, vuelve a ellas para dar continuo aumento a su fecundidad. Allí cada soldado será un héroe porque peleará en defensa de su patria que es feliz y le hace feliz: cada hombre de estado será un Solón, porque fundará su gloria en el poder incontrastable de su país, poder que no tiene otro cimiento que la prosperidad pública. Cada magistrado será un Arístides, porque sabrá que en la rectitud, acierto y pureza de su administración ha de estribar el concierto del orden público: cada ciudadano será un hijo fiel que se interesará en la felicidad de su madre, por conocer que cuanto más prospere ésta, tanto más se acrecentará su patrimonio y con tanta mayor seguridad gozará. Así unidos los conatos de todos para fortalecer el nudo político que los liga, no habrá guerra que los intimide, calamidad que los empobrezca, infortunio que los abata, rivalidad que los aniquile. La roca del estado, apoyada en los cimientos robustos del amor a la patria, resistirá inmóvil el ímpetu de las tempestades más horrendas; y mientras perseveren los cimientos, contrastará la violencia de las olas, y en el día de la serenidad aparecerá grande y triunfante en medio del mar ya tranquilo. Jamás puede llegar a ser infeliz una nación donde se trabaje y el trabajo viva favorecido, y el trabajo será siempre favorecido en cualquier parte donde el amor a la patria sea el móvil de la política y forme el carácter civil de los ciudadanos.[51]

The techniques which Forner uses in this passage are obvious. The cumulative effect of parallel structures is rhythmically important, and the main clauses seem to yield a mathematical form. There are also other sound-patterns which increase the impact of the prose on the senses. There is assonance, for example in 'las poblaciones brillan/las generaciones se multiplican', and the first of these phrases is a regular heptasyllable and the second a hendecasyllable. In the phrase 'refluyen a la patria en nueva y duplicada requeza' there is assonance in A-A (patria/duplicada) and E-A (nueva/riqueza). Forner, in fact, had learnt his Ciceronian lessons well. Yet he makes the style his own, and we should not mistake the more impassioned, metaphoric, vehement handling of Forner's argument with Jovellanos's restraint, though we might have more difficulty in distinguishing Jovellanos from Olavide on the same subject, or from Capmany (1742-1813), Cadalso, Meléndez Valdés, or the conde de Cabarrús. Cadalso, Jovellanos, and Meléndez also use verse rhythms in their prose, but are less free in their metaphors than Forner. Meléndez is more given to the use of assonance than any of the others.[52]

Out of the type of prose written by Forner and Meléndez later writers forged the passionate rhetoric of the Peninsular War period, in which emotion is as central to content as to language. A fine example is the anonymous *Elogio fúnebre de los valencianos que murieron en defensa de su patria la tarde del 28 de junio de 1808* (Cádiz, 1809). The author of this work (one of the Villanueva brothers, perhaps)[53] begins with concepts of an ordered universe and the brotherhood of man which explain his hatred of war: '¿Por ventura una misma razón y unas mismas necesidades no reúnen a los mortales de todos los siglos bajo una misma ley? Sólo pues hay una familia y sólo un pueblo'.[54] Man in his heart, the writer suggests, knows the order of things, and the prose clearly seeks to reflect not merely traditional eloquence but a sense of this basic importance of feeling and emotion as well as reason.

These are also important features of late eighteenth-century novels in Spain. Pedro Montengón's (1754-1821) novels, for instance, make many concessions to the pleasures of the imagination. Although his most famous novel *Eusebio* based its morality on reason rather than on metaphysics, and was attacked by the Inquisition for its conception of fate and its religious tolerance,[55] its plot appealed strongly to the senses, with love, shipwreck, and a North American setting. The same is true of *La Eudoxia* and *El Mirtilo*. The central subjects of the former, an historical novel about the daughter of Belisarius, are the education of women and the proper evaluation of wealth and status, but these are presented in the context of emotional situations arising from the love of Eudoxia for Maximio bearing on the basic topic of the control of the passions by reason. *El Mirtilo* goes even further in its appeal to the senses since it is a pastoral novel with the traditional mixture of poetry and prose. Digressions on population and sheep-rearing problems and on luxury give a certain eighteenth-century spice to the conventional Stoic themes, but there are also highly imaginative and stimulating situations at the end of the novel when Mirtilo comes upon a mother and her beautiful daughter, living in a state of nature in a cave in a lost valley.

The importance of imagination and the passions reached a new height in the 1790s with the publication of Mor de Fuentes's *El cariño perfecto o los amores de Alfonso y Serafina*, later called *La Serafina*. Mor de Fuentes (1762-1848) was familiar with the exploitation of emotional situations in other European writers. He had read Goethe's *Werther*, Rousseau's *La nouvelle Héloïse*, and learnt the lessons of Richardson's *Clarissa*, to which he makes a number of allusions in *La Serafina*.[56] There is also a link between his novel and the *Menosprecio de corte* tradition in Spanish literature, still appealed to in the eighteenth century to encourage landowning *hidalgos* to work on their country estates rather than waste their wealth on anti-social luxuries.

The main topic of the book is love in the provinces, told in the form of letters from Alfonso to his friend Eugenio.[57] Against the power of money to influence parental feeling it sets the primacy of true affection. But it extends the case for the affections by showing their social utility (as opposed to greed and vanity which destroy society), on lines which remind the reader of the poetry of Meléndez, Cienfuegos, and Quintana.[58] Apart from singing the virtues of un-corrupt country life and simple people—the pomp and luxuries of cities breed promiscuous marqueses and venereal disease—Mor de Fuentes evolves a philosophy in the novel which is close to that of Leandro Fernández de Moratín and other Enlightenment writers. Basically, Mor agrees with Pope's *Essay on Man* that man is moti-vated by self-love (*Carta* 64). Self-love can, however, be made social provided that human passions are channelled by reason to be useful rather than destructive. Like Moratín, Mor de Fuentes sees education and reason as the main forces for good; religion has little or no place in the novel. Prostitution is the result of 'falta de educación' in women and men; man needs 'crianza para enfrenar sus arrebatos, amansar su fiereza y suavizar su natural y desabrida selvatiquez' and without it he is 'más feroz e insociable que los mismos irracionales' (*Cartas* 136 and 114; see also 135). The style itself reflects concern with these civilising values. Since the expression of emotion is a sign of compassion for one's fellow-humans and the brotherhood of man, sensibility is vital for literature—'requisito esencialísimo, o más bien indispensable, para el cabal desempeño de toda composición aun cuando sea en prosa' (*Carta* 7). Art, in fact, civilises. How great would Aragon be, Alfonso argues in *Carta* 84, 'si las Artes, y en especial la Poesía, que debe ser la civilizadora de las naciones, hubieran labrado su espíritu'.

Because Mor de Fuentes associates art with feeling, individuality and originality too are important to him in literature. He looks 'n *Carta* 8 for writing which reflects 'cierta gallardía original, como los árboles y demás objectos preeminentes de la Naturaleza'. And of course he is not alone in this. There are social and political, as well as purely literary, reasons no doubt for this renewed interest in originality. We find it in poets and dramatists such as Cienfuegos and Quintana, and abundantly in an artist like Goya. Signs of it can also be traced in a number of discourses in, of all places, the Real Academia de San Fernando, but none perhaps more eloquent than that of José Luis Munárriz, the translator of Blair, at the prize-giving in 1802. Munárriz expressed the aspiration of artists and writers to be lamps rather than mirrors at the period in the following words:

> In reality, to put life into pictures, the Imagination must hold the brush and the Heart must guide it. The Spirit must find joyous images . . . and the Heart, which alone knows how to appeal to the Heart, must strike chords which will arouse our sympathies and our feelings . . . You need a great measure of strength of purpose and wariness to avoid being slavish imitators! The arts cannot progress by imitation alone. Had we never gone further than that we should still be sailing on rafts . . . Those who refuse to invent, and are satisfied with the imitation of the work of others, are feeble in spirit.[59]

NOTES

1. See Fulgencio Afán de Ribera, *Virtud al uso y mística a la moda* (Madrid, 1952), p. 9.
2. Primera Parte, *Visión* VI and *Visión* VII.
3. Segunda Parte, *Visión* XI and *Visión* XII.
4. *El Buscón*, chapter 3, ed. Américo Castro (Madrid, CC, 1960), pp. 32-3.
5. Torres Villarroel, *Visiones y visitas de Torres con Don Francisco de Quevedo por la corte*, ed. Russell P. Sebold (Madrid, CC, 1966), p. 28.
6. For a more detailed discussion of the grotesque in Torres see Paul Ilie, 'Grotesque portraits in Torres Villarroel', *BHS*, XLV (1968), 16–37.
7. In the *Preámbulo* the candle is personified to make an emblem of human life. The candle 'ha días que padece achaques de caduco, destilaciones y gota, males viejos en candil de astrólogo, que como estudia a luz más derecha, tiene mal cuidada la torcida, estuve anoche aguantando la mecha y eneojando a los párpados, que los quiero sobre las niñas de mis ojos, por brujulear las dicciones de un curioso libro que ha meses que le doy mi lado, porque me despierta el sueño'. The word-play is in some instances functional ('destilaciones' and 'gota' are illnesses as well as words appropriate to drips from a wick), but in others seems play for its own sake (the play on 'luz más derecha' and 'mal cuidada la torcida', for example, where the meaning—'because he studies seriously he fails to tend the wick of his lamp'—is not enhanced by paradoxical language). A clear example of wit

which does not extend the meaning is the phrase 'que los quiero sobre las niñas de mis ojos' which, figuratively, means 'I want them more than anything' but applied to 'párpados' ('eyelids') can be taken literally as 'I want them over my eyes'. 'Despertar sueño' is another obvious witticism, with no significance on a more serious level.

8. See 'Carta a un amigo' in Torres Villarroel, *Obras* (Madrid, 1798), XI, 380-82.

9. On Torres's mixed nature and hybrid style see Russell P. Sebold, op. cit., pp. ix-xxxiv.

10. Torres Villarroel, *Vida* (Madrid, CC, 1912), p. 86.

11. For the analysis of the list of subscribers, see below, Appendix A, p. 131.

12. See in general G. Marañón, *Las ideas biológicas del padre Feijoo*, *BAE*, 141, pp. xxxvii *et seq.* His assertion that 'la física experimental . . . es la única que pueda ser útil' occurs in *Paralelo de las lenguas castellana y francesa*, § 2, and there are other references to experiments in *Paradojas matemáticas*, § 5; para. 38 (*BAE*, 141, p. 310). His interest in chemical experiments is reflected in *Examen filosófico de un suceso peregrino de estos tiempos* (*BAE*, 56, p. 456). For Baconian influence on his interest in experiments, see A. Ardao, *La filosofía polémica de Feijóo* (Buenos Aires, 1962), pp. 98 *et seq.*

13. See *BAE*, 141, pp. 205, 208, 211, 215-16, 217, and 317.

14. A. Ardao, op. cit., p. 108.

15. *Consectario a la materia del Discurso antecedente*, § 10, para. 40 (*BAE*, 141, p. 98), and compare also *Duendes y espíritus familiares*, the end of § 1.

16. *Paralelo de las lenguas castellana y francesa*, § 3 (Madrid, CC, 1958), I, 218.

17. ibid., 217.

18. *BAE*, 141, pp. 108-9. Cf. R. Lapesa, 'Sobre el estilo de Feijoo', in *De la edad media a nuestros días* (Madrid, 1967), p. 290.

19. See *Antipatía de franceses y españoles*, § 3, and *BAE*, 141, p. 109.

20. Other techniques to be noted in Feijoo are his occasional use of verse forms in prose, as in the passage '¡Oh piedad mal entendida la de algunos jueces! ¡Oh piedad impía! ¡Oh piedad tirana! ¡Oh piedad cruel!' (*Balanza de Astrea*), where the last three exclamations are hexasyllables and enriched by oxymoron ('piedad cruel' and 'piedad impía'). Balanced sentences also occur in the same essay, as in 'Difícil es . . . tener alma de cera para la vida privada y espíritu de bronce para la administración pública' where the balance is heightened by antitheses (cera/bronce; alma/espíritu; privada/pública). The same essay also provides an example of Feijoo's common use of imagery to sharpen a 'sentencia': 'El alma se marchita con el cuerpo, y son arrugas del alma los encogimientos de la codicia.' It is interesting to compare with the passage from *Honra y provecho* . . . quoted above a more carefully worked-out climax from *Amor de la patria y pasión nacional*, § 6: '¡Cuántos corazones inaccesibles a las tentaciones del oro, insensibles a los halagos de la ambición, intrépidos a las amenaza del poder, se han dejado pervertir míseramente de la pasión nacional.' In this passage each phrase has three elements in parallel. See also R. Lapesa, op. cit., pp. 290-99.

21. See *Glorias de España*, Primera Parte, § 20 (*Teatro crítico universal*,

PROSE 57

Madrid, CC, 1953, II, 148–9). The author's battle for truth can also be found, for example, in *BAE*, 141, p. 109a.

22. For examples of disputatious style see *Respuesta al Dr D. Martin Martínez*, VIII, para. 29 (*BAE*, 141, p. 248), and *Vara divinatoria y zahoríes*, § 4 (*Teatro crítico* . . ., ed. cit. II, 35).

23. For the novelistic sources see Russell P. Sebold's introduction to Vol. I of the Clásicos castellanos ed. (Madrid, 1960), lx *et seq.* For references to Molière in Isla, see ibid., Vol. I, 110, 112–13.

24. For a theory about the treatment of reality in the novel see Russell P. Sebold's Introduction to the Clásicos castellanos ed., pp. lxxiv *et seq.* Sebold's comparison of Isla's technique with that of Zola is a gross oversimplification, however. Isla's novel is by no means documentary in most respects, and its mixture of fiction and reality is very comparable to that of the seventeenth-century novelists.

25. See H. Peterson, 'Notes on the influence of Addison's *Spectator* and Marivaux's *Spectateur français* upon *El Pensador*', *HR*, IV (1936), 256–63.

26. *Pensamiento* XXIII.

27. *Pensamiento* XXIV.

28. *Pensamiento* LV. *Pensamiento* XXXVII ('Sobre la igualdad de fortunas') adopts a traditional Stoic attitude towards fortune in the first half, but has an ironic letter from a poor Indian in the second part which appears to call the validity of the Stoic view into question.

29. The ideas here are similar to those expressed by Cadalso in his *Cartas marruecas*, in *Cartas* LXXI, LXXXIV, LXXV, and LXXXVI (cf. *Cartas marruecas*, ed. cit., pp. xxviii–xxix).

30. See Emily Cotton, 'Cadalso and his foreign sources', in *Liverpool Studies in Spanish Literature*, 1st series (Liverpool, 1940), 1–18; G. Adinolfi, 'Le *Cartas marruecas* di José Cadalso e la cultura spagnola della seconda metà del settecento', in *FR*, III, No. 9 (1956), 30–83; E. F. Helman, 'A note on an immediate source of Cadalso's *Noches lúgubres*', *HR*, XXV (1957), 122–5; Nigel Glendinning, prólogo to ed. of *Noches lúgubres* (Madrid, CC, 1961), pp. xlviii–lxiii.

31. See *Noches lúgubres*, ed. cit., pp. vii–ix, and 'The Traditional Story of "La difunta pleiteada"', Cadalso's *Noches lúgubres* and the Romantics', *BHS*, XXXVIII (1961), 206–15.

32. See *Noches lúgubres*, ed. E. F. Helman (Santander–Madrid, 1951), pp. 43-4 and facsimile document p. 139 (facsimile omitted in 1968 reprint).

33. See José Caso González, 'El comienzo de la reconquista en tres obras dramáticas', *El Padre Feijoo y su siglo* (*CCF*, 18, 1966, III, 505). Professor Caso suggests that Cadalso's 'morofilia' reflects a Spanish Renaissance tradition as well as ideas of the Enlightenment.

34. See *Cartas marruecas*, ed. cit., p. 14.

35. Cadalso, *Defensa de la nación española contra la Carta persiana LXXVIII de Montesquieu*, ed. Guy Mercadier (Toulouse, 1970), p. 9.

36. ibid., p. 15.

37. *Cartas* I–XIV are mostly concerned with Spain and her history; XV, however, with envy; XVI, with the heroic history of Spain; XVII with philosophy and virtue. This kind of alternation of types of topic continues throughout the work and imposes one kind of structure on it.

38. An analysis of sentence structure in the *Apuntaciones autobiográficas* suggests that a high proportion of sentences which do not simply relate actions or events (the vast majority do), are causal.

39. See *Cartas marruecas*, ed. cit., pp. xii-xiii.

40. *El Buscón*, Part I, chapter 8.

41. *Carta* xxxiv, and the prologue of Dupuis and Glendinning's ed., p. xix.

42. See his *Elementos del Cortejo*, republished in a collection of Mexican satires (!) with the title *Sátira anónima del siglo XVIII* (Mexico, 1953), pp. 222-7.

43. In his *Diccionario crítico-burlesco* (Cadiz, 1811; Madrid, 1812 and 1820, etc.).

44. See 'Sátira política inédita del siglo XVIII', in *RCHL*, IV (1899), 500-31.

45. See ed. by Foulché-Delbosc in 'Obras inéditas de Cadalso', *RH*, I (1894), 329-35.

46. Cadalso was a knight of Santiago and was therefore able to prove *hidalguía* on both sides of his family (though he had a minor difficulty on his father's side); Nicolás Fernández de Moratín was 'de familia noble de Asturias' according to his son. The Iriartes could prove *hidalguía* (Bernardo had to for the Order of Charles III); Jovellanos also. Even Ramón de la Cruz's family could be considered 'de condición ahidalgada' according to Cotarelo, although it was financially not well off.

47. *Los literatos en cuaresma por D. Amador de Vera y Santa-Clara* (Madrid, n.d.), first ed., p. 10.

48. See F. López's article in *BH*, LXIX, 26–55.

49. There is no lack of imagery in Navarrete's prose, but attempts to arouse emotion are rare. For an example of the latter cf. his extended sea image in the 'Carta de Lelio Peregrino a Estanislao Borbio' (*BAE*, 25, p. 549b): '¡Cuántos vió la edad pasada, y cuántos ha visto la nuestra, que lisonjeados de la fortuna y no recelando sus inconstancias, se descuidaron en prevenirse para ellas. De que resultó que las plazas que habían sido los teatros de su grandeza fuesen los cadalsos de sus infortunios; porque en este golfo de la privanza se experimentan mayores y más frecuentes tormentas . . .'

50. Jovellanos, *Obras escogidas*, ed. Ángel del Río (Madrid, CC, 1935), I, 156.

51. *Obras de Don Juan Pablo Forner*, recogidas y ordenadas por Don Luis Villanueva, pp. 212-13.

52. In his *Acusación Fiscal contra Basilio C* . . . we find the following climax sentence: 'Las personas se ven atropelladas, los caminos públicos salteados, las casas allanadas.' The poetic rhythm is obvious: two hendecasyllables followed by a heptasyllable. The assonance pattern is equally evident. 'Atropelladas' and 'allanadas' give a pair of AA assonances and there is internal 'rhyme' in the last 'line'.

53. In the 'Advertencia' the author explains that he was with 'el mejor de los magistrados y más tierno y fiel de los amigos' in Seville at the beginning of the Peninsular War; he also speaks of the Valencians as 'mis compatriotas'. The 'magistrate' referred to must be Jovellanos, who was certainly a friend of the Villanueva brothers and with Joaquín in Seville,

according to the latter's autobiography. The Villanuevas came from Játiva and so were 'compatriotas' of the Valencians. They were also in Cadiz when the *Elogio júnebre* was printed. (See Joaquín Lorenzo de Villanueva, *Vida literaria* (London, 1825), I, chapter xix.)

54. ibid, p. 20.

55. See Ángel González Palencia, 'Pedro Montengón y su novela "El Eusebio" ', in *Entre dos siglos* (Madrid, 1943), pp. 137-80.

56. See Ildefonso-Manuel Gil's prologue to his edition of *La Serafina* (Saragossa, 1959), pp. 11-13. Gil fails to note the probable impact of Richardson's work to which there is a concrete reference in *Carta* 112 (ed. cit., p. 147). On Richardson's popularity see Cándido María Trigueros, *Mis pasatiempos*, I (Madrid, 1804), xv.

57. There are 144 letters from Alfonso in all and their chronology helps to bring out the emotional patterns of the book. The periodicity of the letters is between five and eight a month on average, spread over a year and a half from 2 August 1786 to 6 April 1788. In March 1787, however, there are ten, and sixteen in August 1787, including three letters written on 20 August, at a climactic moment in the affair.

58. See Chapter 3, esp. p. 80, below. On the influence of love, cf. *Carta* 118 (ed. cit., p. 156). A further resemblance between Mor, Meléndez, and Cienfuegos and Quintana lies in their concern for the poorer classes. In Mor's novel, a particularly strong criticism of class structure occurs in *Carta* 45 (ibid., p. 79); there is criticism of the anti-social 'caciques' in *Carta* 123 (ibid., p. 161); and sympathy for the needs of the 'clase ínfima' in *Carta* 139 (ibid., p. 187).

59. *Distribución de los premios . . . de la Real Academia de San Fernando . . . de 24 de Julio de 1802*, pp. 86, 94.

Chapter 3

EIGHTEENTH-CENTURY POETRY

RELEVANCE, UTILITY, AND THE PLEASURES of the senses are the major preoccupations of the eighteenth-century poetic theorists. 'Aprovechar deleitando' is the aim of poetry in Luzán's terms.[1] This is in part merely a reaffirmation of Horace's 'Dulce et utile', although it also extends the Classical ideal. The artist should ultimately subordinate art to politics, namely to the common good.[2] Yet, strictly speaking, political utility is rare in eighteenth-century Spanish poetry as we shall see, and a broader usefulness lay in the imitation of *nature*—a term which included the ideal as well as the real world, the abstract as well as the concrete. Utility is in fact a vague concept at the beginning of the century. Pedro Miguel de Samper in his *Aprobación* for a collection of poems by Joseph Tafalla Negrete considered their 'great usefulness' to consist in their comparability with 'los énfasis heroicos de Góngora, . . . las dulces suavidades de Lope, . . . las provechosas moralidades de los Leonardos'[3]—a usefulness which appears in the imitation of Lope and Góngora to be as much a question of style as of content.

The heroic style of Góngora, far from seeming useful in the later eighteenth century, ultimately became an object of utter opprobrium. But it was greatly admired in the first half of the century and widely imitated then, though seventeenth-century critical attitudes to his work persisted. Andalusian writers naturally had the strongest allegiance to his work as a whole. Baroque taste was particularly strong in that part of the peninsula in all the arts. Mansilla (d. after 1730), writing in Córdoba in 1718, felt there was a marked difference of character between the poetic language of Andalusia and the rest of Spain at that period. 'Andalusian prosody,' he wrote, 'is very vehement and much dierisis is made; this is the opposite of the Castilian, which is very smooth and makes much synaeresis.'[4]

The vehemence to which León y Mansilla refers often extends from the mere sound of words to their use and to the concepts they embody, in Andalusian poets of the late seventeenth and early eighteenth centuries. Gabriel Álvarez de Toledo (1662-1714), a Sevillian, has, for example, an obvious taste for involved metaphor, Classical allusion, and hyperbaton, which can be used for parody of the heroic style, as in *La Burromaquia,* as aptly as for the style itself. In his serious *Romance endecasílabo* on the martyrdom of St Lawrence the saint is described in successive lines as 'inocente reo' (oxymoron), 'fiscal sagrado de su juez enorme' (metaphors and conceits—the saint as advocate for God, although criminal victim, as it were, at the same time, to those who martyr him), and when he speaks,

> Con la llama ardorosa de sus labios
> Más articula rayos que razones[5]

(metaphors: flames/lips; thunderbolts/words; and word-play: flames articulate, 'rayos'/'razones').

The conde de Torrepalma (1706-67), who came from Granada, used the Gongoristic manner to such effect that he was nicknamed 'the difficult one' ('El Difícil') when he joined the Academia de Buen Gusto in Madrid in the middle of the century.[6] José Antonio Porcel (1715-94), also from Granada, takes from Góngora's *Soledades* and *Polifemo* the idea of a brilliant and complex-patterned surface beneath which lie for the attentive reader moral and theological truths.

The chief difference between these followers of Góngora in the eighteenth century and their seventeenth-century master appears to lie in the poor quality of their invention (many of their metaphors are borrowed direct from Góngora), their lack of musical sense, and their general inability, with a few exceptions, to sustain the heroic style and preserve a unity of feeling as successfully as Góngora. This is certainly the case in León y Mansilla's *Soledad Tercera,* where Góngora's themes, characteristic imagery, and tricks of style are imitated, sometimes pleasingly enough, but without Góngora's brilliance, density, or variety.

León y Mansilla
Dosel formando de sus ramas bellas,
Y cortina en sus hojas esmaltadas,

A cuyo pie, lascivas no, serpientes,
Sí de cristal, hermosas le ceñían,
Que bordando en espumas
Las que el prado alentó flores hermosas,
Eran de blancas plumas
Nevados cisnes, o canoras rosas.[7]

Góngora

Lo cóncavo hacía de una peña
a un fresco sitial dosel umbroso
y verdes celosías unas yedras,
trepando troncos y abrazando piedras.[8]

Vagas cortinas de volantes vanos
corrió Favonio lisonjeramante,
a la de viento—cuando no sea cama
de frescas sombras—de menuda grama.[9]

In the León y Mansilla passage we have one example of the A no/sí B construction which is typically Gongorine, and one more or less bipartite or *bimembre* line ('Nevados cisnes/ o canoras rosas'). There is a Góngora-type hyperbaton—'Las que el prado alentó flores hermosas' for 'las flores hermosas que el prado alentó', and some internal assonances in O-A (*hojas, hermosas, hermosas*—again!—*canoras, rosas*). *Formando, bordando, prado,* and *nevados* give another set, in A-O. The 'curtain of enamelled leaves' is a rather clumsily mixed metaphor, although the idea of the water embroidering in spray the reflection of the flowers in the field, and not knowing whether this made snow-white swans or singing roses of white feathers, is a not unpleasing conceit. The music of the passage is decidedly less effective. There is great variety of stress pattern from line to line, yet no very evident rhythmic effect ensues. 'Las que el prado alentó flores hermosas' is particularly uneven at the beginning; and so is the second line although it is basically dactylic. The large number of pairs of adjectives and nouns in the same order in successive lines (ramas bellas/hojas esmaltadas; blancas plumas/nevados cisnes/canoras rosas) gives a tuneless monotony compared with the pleasing variety of stress and order in the 'fresco sitial dosel umbroso/ y verdes celosías' of Góngora. The more or less *bimembre* is less satisfying than the perfect *bimembre* of Góngora ('de frescas sombras,

de menuda grama'). Finally, León has nothing to compare even
remotely with the rich sonorities of 'vagas cortinas de volantes vanos'
nor with the alliterated line with repeated structures and internal
rhyme 'trepando troncos y abrazando piedras'.

León y Mansilla clearly knew his Góngora well. His *Soledad* fits
into one of the patterns for four *Soledades* attributed to Góngora, the
four ages of man; he also appreciated the value of tonal contrasts and
shared Góngora's desire to appeal to a minority.[10] Indeed, many of
the eighteenth-century imitators of Góngora seem to have worked in
and for small, select, and mainly aristocratic circles. The conde de
Torrepalma and José Antonio Porcel—the one a legitimate noble, the
other illegitimate[11]—belonged first to the Academia del Trípode in
Granada and later joined the Academia del Buen Gusto which met at
the house of the marqués de Sarria in Madrid. The choice of the
Hunting Eclogue form by Porcel for his major poetic work *El Adonis*,
dictated by the Granada group, also legitimised minority language
and aristocratic setting, since 'as it is a hunting eclogue, and those
who speak are huntsmen, who can be kings or princes even, people
with a good education and not merely countryfolk, erudite references
and elevated language are not out of place.'[12]

Perhaps the most original imitator of Góngora, if there can be
originality in imitation, is Porcel, in whose work there are also echoes
of Garcilaso. A comparison with Garcilaso and Góngora in his case
reveals not so much weaknesses of poetic invention and technique as
differences of conception. It is instructive to compare the poetic contest between Prócris and Anaxarte in the first eclogue of Porcel's
El Adonis with the amœban song of Alcino and Tirreno in the third
eclogue of Garcilaso.

Garcilaso

Tirreno:

Flérida, para mí dulce y sabrosa
más que la fruta del cercado ajeno,
más blanca que la leche y más hermosa
que'l prado por abril, de flores lleno;
si tú respondes pura y amorosa
al verdadero amor de tu Tirreno,
a mi majada arribarás, primero
que'l cielo nos amuestre su lucero.

Alcino:

Hermosa Filis, siempre yo te sea
amargo al gusto más que la retama,
y de ti despojado yo me vea,
cual queda el tronco de su verde rama,
si más que yo el murciélago desea
la escuridad, ni más la luz desama,
por ver ya el fin de un término tamaño
deste día, para mí mayor que un año.[13]

Porcel

Prócris:

A aquél que no desea
Del amor la süave tiranía,
No así le lisonjea
La llama en que se abrasa el alma mía,
La llama que saldrá del pecho tarde.
¡Tan dulcemente en sus cuidados arde!

Anaxarte:

Tan crüelmente en sus cuidados arde
Quien de Amor atrevido
Fía, inocente, el corazón cobarde,
Que siente sin sentido.
Si las glorias de amor traen estos daños,
Mal hayan sus engaños.[14]

A detailed look at these two passages of Porcel and Garcilaso shows up some very sharp differences. In the first place Porcel generalises while Garcilaso's shepherds sing of their own particular cases. Rhythmically the Garcilaso stanzas are much more regular than those of Porcel, although the last line of Alcino's stanza is in fact a dodecasyllable (12 syllables) and not hendecasyllabic. Accents in Tirreno's speech fall more or less regularly on the second, sixth, and tenth syllables (lines 3, 4, 5, 6, and 8), and in Alcino's on the second, fourth, sixth, and tenth (all except the irregular sixteenth line). Although the rhyme-pattern of Porcel's exchange between Anaxarte and Prócris is based on Garcilaso, the stanzas offer more variety and all but two of Porcel's hendecasyllables have a different stress pattern.

They tend to complement one another rather than create a balance of equal elements, and the 'lira'-type mixture of hendecasyllables and heptasyllables varies from one stanza to the next. (Garcilaso stanza 1: ABABABCC; stanza 2: DEDEDEFF. Porcel stanza 1: aBaBCC; stanza 2: cdcdEe.) There is less rigour in the pattern of accentuation in Porcel, and the whole section reflects an interest in rapid contrasts which is very far from Garcilaso. It is not, of course, that Garcilaso (or Góngora for that matter) was not interested in contrasts. Dámaso Alonso has shown how the *Polifemo* is constructed around contrasting dark and light sections,[15] and in Garcilaso's first and second eclogues parallels and contrasts between Salicio and Nemoroso and between Salicio and Albanio (and Albanio and tranquil nature) are enormously important. But in their poetry the contrasts evolve slowly in large-scale patterns. Porcel, on the other hand, seems to prefer a swifter alternation of contrasting sections. Each stanza at the beginning of his first eclogue begins with a line that echoes the end of the previous stanza but reverses its sense (Prócris: 'Tan *dulcemente* . . .' Anaxarte: 'Tan *crüelmente* . . .'). This violent reversal is quite unlike similar exchanges in earlier poets, including Theocritus and Virgil. Furthermore, Porcel does not keep rigidly to the pattern established in the opening stanzas of the exchange. After the third stanza, the fourth (and successive verses) merely pick up the last line of the preceding stanza without modification, and the rhyme-scheme changes to tercets after the first six lines of the eighth stanza.

This variety of Porcel could be explained by a lack of technical skill, but an analysis of the whole group of eclogues suggests that variety is of the essence and not merely accidental.

The basic unity of the four eclogues Porcel calls *El Adonis* lies in the story of Venus and Adonis itself, parts of which are related in each of the four poems. There are other unifying elements: the hunting descriptions which occur in each, and the style of language of course, but also the vicissitudes in love of the two huntresses whose own story as well as that of Adonis is related in the eclogues—Prócris and Anaxarte. These central stories all have the same theme: the inevitable tragedy of love which leads to jealousy and to the rejection of chastity. They are all, furthermore, stories from Ovid's *Metamorphoses*, particularly Books VII and X. Some of the eclogues refer to other and related Classical legends with similar overtones of the misfortunes attendant on the passions. And there is in fact a build-up of supporting evidence, as it were, over the four eclogues. In the first eclogue we have Prócris and Anaxarte themselves, and Anaxarte begins to relate the story of Venus and Adonis. In the second, Prócris recalls briefly the sad consequences of passion in Helen, Theseus, Medea, Europa, Proserpina, Ciane, and Ceres, and describes in more detail a plate (*lámina*) illustrating the tale of Boreas and Oritia. In the third eclogue Oritia's legend returns and the stories of Pirene, Cencreo, and Mirra are related at length. And in the fourth and final eclogue the lovers of Anaxarte and Prócris—Céfalo and Ifis—join the two huntresses, and the climax of their stories and the end of the Venus, Adonis, and Pirene tale are narrated, with subsections about Circe and Pico.

The set of eclogues, therefore, provides variety in itself: variations on a theme, in fact, each of the four having more variations than the last. Each has a slightly different poetic structure, as well as a varied narrative line, although a certain pattern predominates, giving unity to the whole. In all the eclogues, Porcel seems to follow the pattern of Garcilaso's second eclogue in a general way: *terza rima* is the basic metre, with sections of *canción* and *silva* for contrast. *Silva* is always used for the Venus and Adonis story, and in the long *silva* section in the first eclogue there is a tighter subsection rather reminiscent of the 'Oh, bienaventurado albergue' passage in Góngora's *Soledad Primera*.[16] In the second eclogue, five stanzas of *canción* from Procris open the eclogue, *tercetos* follow until the narrative of the Venus and Adonis story is resumed in *silvas*, and a short group of *tercetos* then round the eclogue off. Once again, as in the first eclogue, there is a subsection within the Adonis narration. Venus relates a series of parallel stories of tragic love (Jacinto, Orion, Acteon, Narciso, and Cipariso) in *silva* fragments of varied but balancing proportions (12, 18, 26, 11, and 11 lines respectively). The similar pattern of the third eclogue gives sections of *canción, terza rima, silva* (for the Adonis story), and *terza rima* again. The fourth eclogue is not much different; *octavas, tercetos, silva* (for the Venus and Adonis section), and *tercetos* again to conclude. In the third and fourth eclogues there is nothing quite comparable to the subsections of the Venus and Adonis narrative in the first two eclogues, but there are reported speeches of Pirene, Adonis, and Venus in the third, and many reported speeches (and speeches within speeches) in the final eclogue, all creating separate foci of interest and providing sources of dramatic tension.

The general impression of balance and tension which this analysis provides is strengthened by other details. In the first eclogue, for instance, a description of a hunt in the Venus and Adonis section flows naturally on into the Prócris and Anaxarte framework. There are echoes of the first eclogue in the second, not merely on the narrative level; the descriptions at the beginning of the Venus and Adonis section open in very similar ways in both eclogues, and there are parallel descriptions of rabbits, hares, and other game in both.[17] The third eclogue's opening exchange between Anaxarte and Prócris is a piece of 'canto amebeo' similar to that in the first eclogue and uses an identical device of repetition of the last lines of one stanza in the first line of the next. And the fourth eclogue begins with another such exchange between Céfalo and Ifis with the same contrasts of mood and language-play as in the song contest in the first eclogue.

All these points amply confirm Orozco's contention that Porcel's poem reflects a similar aesthetic to that of the buildings of his period, where variety of detail within a unified conception is common. The Porcel eclogues might also be compared with Hipólito Rovira Brocandel's porch for the house of the marqués de Dos Aguas in Valencia, or Narciso Tomé's *transparente* for the cathedral of Toledo. Both these works have an overall symbolic unity—the title of the marqués (Dos Aguas), his estates, and the patronage of the Virgin of the Rosary in the first case; and the Mass, its institution, significance, and Old Testament parallels in the second. Both, moreover, have a profusion of detail and an interest in contrasts and striking effects: Tomé's apparently peelable columns, for instance, and Rovira's alabaster water. Above all they are theatrical. And what could be more theatrical than Porcel's poem, totally caught up as it is in the world of Classical legend and Arcady (unlike Garcilaso and Góngora), and only reaching out to the reader/audience through situation and the occasional generalisation?

The public which Porcel envisaged for this poem was clearly, in the first instance, a small aristocratic intellectual élite. At the same time the subject of the poem has a general moral relevance—chastity and the hard path of true love—even if the handling is obviously élitist. Many of the followers of Góngora, and not merely those who had a sort of vested Andalusian interest in the style, wrote essentially minority verse. Apart from those mentioned already, Gerardo Lobo (1670-1750), for instance, was a great producer of occasional poetry,[18] whose wit, equally occasional, saves him perhaps from total oblivion. Like Álvarez de Toledo he used the heroic style in parodies such as his *Octavas festivas a la derrota de unos pasteles en el Palau*, as well as in poems whose subjects—the siege of Lérida and the taking of Orán, for example—immediately suggested such treatment. But like writers of heroic religious poetry such as Padre Butrón y Múxica (b. 1677) and Pedro Nolasco de Ozejo, Lobo borrowed only decorative elements from Góngora and not his sense of overall structure, and one can easily understand how the style came to be criticised for hollowness and irrelevance.[19]

The reaction against the followers of Góngora (continuing the seventeenth-century opposition from critics like Jáuregui, Cascales, and Quevedo) first begins to make itself felt in the eighteenth century with Gregorio Mayans (1699-1781) in the 1720s. The attack on followers of Góngora soon switched to the work of the master himself. The reviewer of Pedro Nolasco's *El sol de los anacoretas, la luz de Egypto*, in the 1737 volume of the *Diario de los literatos de España*, suggests that Góngora's imitators 'sólo consiguieron desacreditar a su inventor, y hacerse objetos de la risa y el desprecio'.[20] And in the same year, the first edition of Luzán's *Poética* made particularly strong and sweeping attacks on Góngora. In 1748, Gómez Arias in the prologue to his *Descripción harmónica de la vida y milagros de . . . S. Antonio de Padua* attacks those who continue to write religious poetry in the 'culto' manner, asserting that 'un estilo muy claro, muy natural y muy ajeno de toda afectación' ought to be used in such poems, 'con frases inteligibles para todos'.[21]

Even within circles of friends opinion was divided sharply on this issue. At the private academy 'del Buen Gusto' in Madrid in the 1750s Luzán, the marqués de Valdeflores (1722-73), and Montiano were anti-Góngora, Porcel and José de Villarroel for him. Both sides were aware of the criticism of excessive metaphor and obscurity in Spanish levelled by writers in other European countries, and no doubt this contributed to the more general swing towards Neo-classical ideals in the second half of the century. But the early proponents of Neo-classicism were not devoid of influence. If their books were not widely read they could propagate their ideas through the Royal Academies to which they belonged. Valdeflores dated the revival of 'good taste' in

Spanish poetry from the founding of the Real Academia Española in 1714,[22] and their involvement in the newly created Real Academia de San Fernando in the 1750s is plain to see. Juan de Iriarte (1702-71), Montiano, and Luzán were academicians; the conde de Torrepalma and the marqués de Sarria (at whose house the Academia del Buen Gusto met), councillors. Yet it is doubtful whether Neo-classicism could really have spread had it not been taught in the schools as well, particularly by the Jesuits.[23]

A pupil of the Society of Jesus, Nicolás Fernández de Moratín (1737-80), was the first to establish himself as a poet in the next generation. His periodical *El Poeta* began to appear in 1764, and each number contained a variety of poems in different forms and styles. Moral poems, both pastoral and satirical, predominate in the elder Moratín's production, and the form of publication itself suggests the author's desire to be useful to society. He expresses this intention most clearly in an anacreontic which appeared in the third issue of *El Poeta*.[24] Imagining himself getting ready to write amorous poetry or heroic verse celebrating Spanish victories, he describes how the Muse invites him to deal with a still more heroic enterprise—the cleaning-up of Madrid:

> Mas si aspirar pretendes
> A empresas más heroicas,
> Limpia a Madrid del vicio
> Cual Juvenal a Roma.
> Con satírico verso,
> Que al suyo contrapongas,
> Ridiculiza el vicio,
> Y haz la virtud famosa.
> Destierra el ocio infame,
> Y extravagancias todas,
> A que por su capricho
> Los hombres se abandonan.
> Sólo así serás digno
> Del cristal de Beocia
> Y así sólo en Parnaso
> Se adquiere la corona.[25]

Spanish society at the time was going through a period of self-criticism and reassessment. People's rights and the pattern of government were being widely discussed, and there was a growing awareness of the ideas being expressed elsewhere in Europe. The economic situation was still so uncertain that a bad harvest and a rise in the price of bread could lead to disturbances in many parts of the country.[26] In Feijoo's time when the harvest had failed, starving people poured into the cities and died on the streets. In 1766, when the crop was poor, the Esquilache riots broke out in Madrid and in many provincial capitals.

Moratín records the ferment of ideas in some of his poems, particularly in the satires:

> Disputa el labrador sobre la armada;
> Juzga el soldado, por qué fue su vida
> Sólo en vender cigarros empleada,
> Que puede gobernar la esclarecida
> Ibera monarquía, que ha dejado
> El cielo al grande Carlos sometida.
> El mercader, que está desocupado
> Desde su mostrador con magisterio
> El consejo gobierna y el estado;
> Pone severa ley al ministerio
> Y trata con despego y sin caricia
> A los hombres más grandes del imperio.[27]

The attitude behind this satire is clearly conservative or reactionary, in favour of law and order and the preservation of a strong monarchy and government upholding traditional values. Moratín extols similar values in patriotic poems such as 'Las naves de Cortés destruidas', poems on royal or academic occasions, the eclogue 'A Velasco y González', poems to Spanish generals and political leaders, *romances* on subjects from Spanish history, and the 'Empresa de Micer Jaques Borgoñón'. His attitude to bull-fighting in the *Carta histórica sobre las fiestas de toros* is equally traditionalist, and the sport is seen as an expression of the courage and austerity of aristocratic Spaniards in the past, qualities which he wishes to revive. The poem to the bull-fighter Pedro Romero has a similar theme, as do the *Quintillas* titled as 'Fiestas de Toros en Madrid'. In the didactic poem on hunting dedicated to the Infante Don Luis—*La Diana*—written early in the 1760s, he argues for the control of society by a powerful but prudent monarch. The people are like cannons, he argues, 'la piedad y política apacibles/contienen a los dos'.[28]

At the same time several progressive Enlightenment topics find their way, incidentally, into *La Diana*. Notable among these is an interest in experimental science and physics, which Moratín associates with Feijoo and sees as helping to drive false beliefs and values out of Spain at the end of the final Canto.[29] In the first Canto he speaks of his interest in inquiries into the nature of human life and the universe; in the second asserts the importance of scientific knowledge and training to the prince; and in the third criticises views of natural phenomena which the superstitious see as portents. These scientific passages form part of a larger theme in the poem; that of Reason. In Canto VI hunting is seen as a worthy exercise for man because it overcomes the irrational:

> Esta es de los campeones digna hazaña,
> Limpiar de monstruos bárbaros el mundo
> Como Alcides: del hombre la alta saña
> La razón vence con pensar profundo;
> Mas las fieras que en cóleras exceden
> Matan sin más razón, que porque pueden.[30]

At the same time Moratín says nothing to conflict with religious beliefs. The Copernican system for him, as for Feijoo and Luzán,[31] is no more than a hypothesis to be placed on the same footing as Ptolemaic theory. Thus in the first Canto he asks whether the sun 'está inmóvil, o en torno es volteado'; and he rejects the atomic theories of Lucretius and Epicurus who attribute the order of the universe to chance in favour of a God-centred system in Canto III. Yet the view he expresses of an ordered universe is not always so orthodox. And in his long poem *El arte de las putas*, which circulated in manuscript in the 1770s, and was put on the Index by the Inquisition in 1777,[32] he makes some much more audacious statements.

In the first instance Moratín's *Arte* . . . accepts man's sexual urges as a part of his nature, even though opposed to some of the virtues. Virtue indeed, he argues, may not always be a good thing from the point of view of human society; orthodox morality can be inhuman. The point emerges very clearly in a passage on chastity in the first Canto:

> ¡Castidad! Gran virtud que el cielo adora,
> virtud de toda especie destructora,
> y si los brutos y aves la observaran

comiéramos de viernes todo el año:
pero, ¿por qué abrazar el Himeneo?
Muchos en los demás escarmentados
le aborrecen tenaces, pues templados
no son los hombres, ni templarse pueden
si no quebrantan la naturaleza
con muy duro y con áspero castigo,
que es inhumanidad si no es fiereza,
de la ley natural dogma enemigo
y no puede haber hombre si es humano
que lo deje de ser . . .[33]

Elsewhere in the poem Moratín wittily justifies the subject of his *Arte* by pointing out the relative harmlessness to human society of prostitution when compared with common subjects of epic poetry such as war.[34]

This and other poems of Moratín are as interesting musically as they are thematically. The last passage, for instance, has examples of internal assonance as well as rhyme, using couplets occasionally. Moratín was not alone in believing in the importance of musicality in poetry. In an exchange of letters with Cadalso the possibility of achieving in Spanish effects comparable with those of Latin poetry was discussed.[35] And Moratín certainly revived experimentation with Sapphics in Spain, following the imitations of Horace's odes made in the seventeenth century by Quevedo and Villegas. Yet in Moratín's and Cadalso's poetry the imitation of the Classics is very different from the Classicism of the earlier generation such as Porcel or Luzán. The latter adopted Classical formulae or put on stagey Classical dress, whereas Moratín and Cadalso, at their best, seem rather to have *lived* in the Classical manner, accepting the values as well as the forms. Certainly in their anacreontics the praise of retirement, wine, and love as a morally better way of life than war or ambition seems to have been felt, indeed experienced, in the company of 'Dorisa', 'Filis', and their friends, rather than merely advocated. The pastoral world of these poems is not truly Arcadian so much as Madrilenian. After all, Madrid was much more rural in the eighteenth century than it is today.

Poetry expressing personal emotions was of course nothing new, but Moratín's generation (García de la Huerta, Cadalso, Tomás de

Iriarte) seem to bring to poetry a new emotional intensity which, for all their rhetoric, is more direct than Álvarez de Toledo, Torrepalma, or the other members of the private academies of the earlier part of the century. Possibly the explanation is to be found in the respective lives of the writers, all of whom experienced the official change in attitude to literature after the Esquilache riots, and whose main protector, the conde de Aranda, fell from favour in 1772. Possibly the cult of feeling in European literature at the period—the 'comédie larmoyante' in France, for example—had something to do with it. Three of these poets—Moratín, Huerta, and Cadalso—also themselves suffered a fall from favour. Moratín and Cadalso were both banished from the Court, and Huerta was actually imprisoned, first in Madrid and later in Orán.[36]

The personal element finds its clearest expression in Cadalso, whose prologue to his *Ocios de mi juventud* states that all his poems were written 'when some motive for sorrow struck me, perhaps the result of my many misfortunes, or of my youth, or perhaps of the combination of the two'.[37] A concern with the sincerity of his poetry is also evident. He says that in the only heroic subject he has treated he was not motivated by a desire to flatter the person in question (he must be referring to the poem 'A los días del Excmo. Conde de Ricla') and asserts that 'my pen has followed no other voice than that of my heart'. In dealing with patriotic subjects too, Cadalso claims that he has tried to speak 'with all the zeal I feel towards my country, and with all the justice that history does it'. This preoccupation with sincerity and with poetry as 'relief for my suffering' does not, however, mean that Cadalso's work is just an outpouring of his feelings and emotions purely for his own satisfaction. A look at his *Ocios* soon convinces the reader that Cadalso, like Luzán, feels that in poetry about love or personal experiences the poet should 'discreetly intermingle many philosophical reflections and moral advice'.[38] Furthermore, one of the most original aspects of Cadalso's collection of poems is its obvious design to make the reader follow a line of argument,[39] leading from the discussion of his reasons for writing poetry and his conceptions of it, at the beginning of the *Ocios*, to the reasons for his renunciation of poetry on the death of 'Filis' at the end. The collection has a clear pattern about it. Instead of putting all the poems of one type together, Cadalso breaks up the main groupings of anacreontics, sonnets, and satirical poems. At certain points a change of direction is clearly announced. After the poem 'Llegóse a mí con el semblante adusto', in whose title it is declared that poetry is 'un estudio frívolo, y convenirme aplicarme a otros más serios', Cadalso turns with ironic aptness to 'Sonetos de una gravedad inaguantable'. Similarly, the anacreontic which follows immediately after the heroic poem 'A los días del Conde de Ricla' begins by rejecting the heroic style: 'Vuelve, mi dulce lira,/Vuelve a tu estilo humilde'. Sensitivity to sequence instilled in the reader by examples such as these, for instance, makes it possible to see the two poems 'Mudanzas de la Suerte' as a generalised comment on fate relevant to the poem they follow on the poet's own adverse fortune, 'Carta escrita desde una aldea de Aragón a Ortelio'.

Cadalso's poetry sought to appeal to the senses as well as to the intelligence. He exploits musical effects and rhetorical structures in the anacreontics, where the very subject of the poem is the world of the senses. Musicality was obviously a major concern at the period, the reader allowing himself to enjoy some lines of a poem more than others without necessarily looking at the context of the whole poem. As Mor de Fuentes wrote, 'de doce literatos o aficionados que lean de buena fe y con inteligencia a Virgilio o a Meléndez, cada uno se impresiona más o menos con sus rasgos, cada uno prefiere o pospone estos o aquellos verses'.[40] The 'Carta escrita desde una aldea de Aragón' shows the importance of sound in the picture of idealised country life:

> Si de otros pastores
> Las danzas presencio
> Advierto mudanzas;
> Y como las temo
> Del pecho que sabes
> El baile aborrezco.
> Si llego a la mesa,
> Es vano el intento
> De probar manjares:
> Ninguno apetezco.[41]

Parallel structures are here emphasised by internal rhyme and assonance (danzas/mudanzas; advierto/pecho/llego). Frequently parallel patterns of sound or language are used in conjunction with such devices as *bimembres* and chiasmus.

Cadalso's model in his anacreontics, one much admired in the eighteenth century for the musicality of his verse, is Villegas.[42] The latter, together with Quevedo, Garcilaso, and Horace, seem to have been the most influential poets from Cadalso's point of view. Cadalso's poetry is in fact less cosmopolitan in inspiration and more limited in theme than his prose works and his drama.

But among Cadalso's contemporaries and younger friends echoes of foreign poets begin to be found. The English poet Edward Young had some influence on Cadalso himself, though the influence of Pope, Thomson, and Milton is more striking in others.[43] Very probably their work aroused interest at this period because of their philosophical and social themes; obviously proper topics for poetry when utility is its main criterion. These influences are exploited in a set of philosophical poems published in Seville in the 1770s by Cándido María de Trigueros which paraphrase Pope's *Essay on Man* in a number of stanzas. The latter was also the model for one of Meléndez Valdés's poems,[44] although there may be echoes of Young in it as well.

It is in Meléndez (1754-1817) that the 'great chain of being' idea, which appears in Pope, Thomson, and Young as well as in many French poets of the period,[45] finds its clearest expression, pointing to an ordered universe which has social as well as scientific implications. Meléndez's philosophical poems join 'la utilidad con el deleite' in Iriarte's terms.[46] In his third poetic *Discurso* Meléndez takes a deeper plunge into modern science than any previous Spanish poet. If Luzán, Moratín, and Cadalso all take Copernican theory as a hypothesis, Meléndez at last seems to accept its validity when he describes how Saturn circles round the sun; and Newtonian gravity explains the comets' movement:

> Yo vi entonces el cielo encadenado;
> Y alcancé a computar por qué camina
> En torno el sol Saturno tan pausado.
>   ¡O Atracción! ¡o lazada peregrina
> Con que la inmensa creación aprieta
> Del sumo Dios la voluntad divina!
>   Tú del crinado, rápido cometa
> Al átomo sutil el móvil eres,
> La ley que firme ser a ser sujeta.[47]

The same system which makes all things in the universe interdependent is elsewhere applied by Meléndez to society. The noble who does not look after those who work for him is a weak link in the great chain of being. Not only is such a noble unvirtuous—a common enough criticism of the noble in earlier periods—but he is also infringing the laws of reason. This emerges very clearly in the satire on the nobility that Meléndez first published in *El Censor*,[48] in which the nobles of the present, living in idle luxury in the cities, are compared unfavourably with those who lived and worked on their estates in the past:

> ¿Son para aquesto señores?
> ¿Para esto vela y afana
> El infelice colono,
> Expuesto al sol y la escarcha?
> Mejor, sí mejor sus canes
> Y las bestias en sus cuadras
> Están. ¡Justo Dios! ¿Son éstas,
> Son éstas tus leyes santas?
> ¿Destinaste a esclavos viles
> A los pobres? ¿de otra masa
> Es el noble que el plebeyo?
> ¿Tu ley a todos no iguala?
> ¿No somos todos tus hijos?
> ¿Y esto ves; y fácil callas?
> ¿Y contra un despota injusto
> Tu diestra al débil no ampara?
> ¡Ah! sepan que con sus timbres
> Y sus carrozas doradas
> La virtud los aborrece,
> Y la razón los infama.
> Sólo es noble ante sus ojos
> El que es útil y trabaja;
> Y en el sudor de su frente
> Su honroso sustento gana.
> Ella busca, y se complace
> Del artesano en la hollada
> Familia; y sus crudas penas
> Con gemidos acompaña.

Allí el triste se conduele
Del triste; y con mano blanda
Le da el alivio, que el rico
En faz cruda le negara.[49]

Much of Meléndez's non-satirical poetry also has a social or
political slant to it. Sometimes this is expressed in a very obvious
way, as in the 'Epístola al Príncipe de la Paz', which supports
Godoy's plans for improving education and the general attempts to
revitalise the agricultural economy with canals, scientific techniques,
and legislation against entailment of estates ('vinculación'). In his
dedication for the Valladolid 1797 edition of his *Poesías*, Meléndez
expresses the hope that Godoy may find many of the poems pleasing
precisely because of his concern for agriculture. To Meléndez, they
were 'composiciones en que he procurado pintar y hacer amables la
vida y los trabajos rústicos, y la inocente bondad de los habitadores
del campo'.[50] To some, this political content was rather unsubtle, and
an anonymous correspondent of the *Diario de Madrid* on 23 December 1798 asked '¿Qué alma cristiana podrá tolerar el desastrado
romance político económico intitulado "La despedida de un anciano"?'
On the other hand, Mor de Fuentes, in his novel *La Serafina*, with a
similar concern to show the desirability of honest country life and to
criticise the commotion and ambitions of the city, makes his protagonist eulogise

el tierno, el armonioso, el castizo Meléndez, que en sus divinos
Romances Pastoriles sabe arrebatar y enloquecer los corazones
inocentes tras los únicos objetos apreciables de la Naturaleza, como
son árboles, flores, arroyos, aves, rebaños.[51]

Meléndez's *romance* 'Los segadores', for example, follows Thomson's
Autumn in urging landowners to be charitable to those who are less
favoured in their circumstances.[52] Other poems—the anacreontics
which eulogise the simple country life, for instance—are only
obliquely a form of propaganda to encourage the wealthy to take a
new interest in rural life, and so to revive the country's agricultural
system according to the doctrines of the Physiocrats.

In these poems, word-music and images are 'useful delights'. Yet
Meléndez's exploitation of the senses is much sharper than that of
earlier eighteenth-century poets. Garcilaso and Luis de León provide
examples which he followed, as did others of his group at

Salamanca:[53] Fray Diego González (1733?-94), who was closer to the sixteenth-century poets in his religious conception of life, and José Iglesias de la Casa (1748-91), whose conception of pastoral is more Classical and moral, and less politically motivated than that of Meléndez. But the world of the senses assumes a new strength in all of these poets. In Iglesias the variety of nature is particularly striking in the *canción* 'La soledad', a poem which contrasts the sublime architecture of nature with the poor efforts of man. The theme is, of course, the traditional moral one of country versus Court, although it is given a slight social twist when Iglesias shows that the Divine Architect works for poor as well as rich while the human architect only works for the latter. The descriptions of landscape are even more varied than those of Porcel, but also more specific and less idealised, and the metaphors are worked into more coherent patterns. The latent aesthetic is that of the picturesque and the sublime, beginning to be fashionable in the landscapes of the period, rather than the symbolic world of the late Baroque: 'confuso amontonar de cosas/ Arrojados acaso y diferentes'; 'varia pintura'; 'natural desorden'.[54] There are echoes of earlier authors and conceptions—'el canto de las aves, *no aprendido*', for instance, which goes back to Luis de León's 'Vida retirada' and his translation of Horace's *Beatus Ille*[55] as well as Cadalso's *Noches lúgubres*; and 'luciente cristal' for a stream, which comes from Góngora.[56] These elements recall the idealised landscape of earlier periods. But Iglesias very often pursues the visual impact of landscape for its own sake: romantic landscape, in fact, in the sense in which Thomson uses the term in his *Seasons*. The sound of the lines also contributes to the beauty of the objects described, mountains, torrents, etc. Indeed all the senses seem to come together in the following passage describing flowers on a hillside:

> Vese del tiempo y humedad cubierta
> La hueca peña de menudas flores,
> Parte en sombras y parte en resplandores,
> Jaspeada aquí, allá verde y allá yerta,
> Formando un todo de hermosura enjerta
> sus metales lucidos
> Y extraños coloridos,
> Y esmaltando la tez que los remata
> De granos de oro y escarchada plata.[57]

Here balanced phrases, as in lines 2, 3, and 9, are enriched with assonances: hueca peña; formando/extraños/esmaltando/granos; escarchada plata.

Meléndez makes an equally intense play with the senses in many of his poems about natural phenomena—flowers, streams, the seasons, and so forth. In his *Romance* xxxiv, 'La tarde', he finds ecstasy in the contemplation of nature, reaching a natural climax in a state of peace:

> Todo es paz, silencio todo,
> Todo en estas soledades
> Me conmueve, y hace dulce
> La memoria de mis males.[58]

Virtually the same concept appears in the *Oda* xiii, 'Al mediodía', in the lines:

> Todo es silencio y paz. ¡Con qué alegría
> Reclinado en la grama
> Respira el pecho, por la vega umbría
> La mente se derrama![59]

His eyes in both poems are 'embebecidos'; sights 'deslumbran'; sounds 'ensordecen'; and the verb 'enajenar' comes into both poems. A sense of climax is reached in 'Al mediodía' (with a pile-up of EO assonances) in the following lines:

> La lluvia, el sol, el ondeante viento,
> La nieve, el hielo, el frío,
> Todo embriaga en celestial contento
> El tierno pecho mío.[60]

In these passages there is a clear difference of emphasis between Meléndez and Iglesias. Meléndez describes the impact of nature on his own senses;[61] Iglesias in the poem discussed generalises about the impact on the senses.

Both Meléndez and Iglesias extend the sensual range of poetry from the world of nature into human and erotic areas, and there are clear links with French sensualist poetry and theory in several instances; in Meléndez's 'El gabinete' (*Oda* vii) for example, 'El retrato' (*Elegía* iv), and in the cycle of poems in a more Classical

Catullan tradition, 'La paloma de Filis'. The conventional anacreontic provides a form with a Spanish tradition on to which another can easily be grafted. And of course the *letrilla* form often used by Quevedo and Góngora to satirise sensuality is frequently used by these writers, notably by Iglesias.

The next generation, particularly Cienfuegos (1764-1809) and Quintana (1772-1857), owed much to Meléndez's example. Cienfuegos wrote a number of early variations on Meléndez's themes. He also had a taste for ironic epigrams which remind one more of Iglesias, and which exploit a similar range of topics, such as social and academic pride: the sardonic obverse of the anacreontic coin.

Like Meléndez, Cienfuegos has a sharp sense of society. The anacreontic vein which seems often to cultivate private virtue, or at best rejects an ambitious society for love's sake, becomes more keenly moral than sensual in Cienfuegos. 'La violación del propósito' sees the poet's love for Laura as the centre of a whole order of things, a universe in itself; yet love is also represented as not only a private delight, but as proof of the brotherhood of man. In 'Mi paseo solitario de primavera' love is the sense of responsibility towards others in the great chain of being:

> . . . hermana al hombre
> Con sus iguales, engranando a aquestos
> Con los seres sin fin.[62]

Lack of love isolates man and breaks 'la trabazón del universo entero'. Later in another poem he subtly plays on the traditional enslavement image of love's chains and the 'great chain of being', referring to love's awakening which

> en su hermanal cadena
> enlaza al hombre recreando el mundo.[63]

Friendship and love in 'El recuerdo de mi adolescencia' are the 'lazo tierno' which binds men together in the sense of the social contract; and 'amor es hermandad' in the poem 'A un amigo en la muerte de un hermano'. The importance of a concern for fellow-humans, particularly those in misfortune, is as sharp in Cienfuegos as in Meléndez or as in Cadalso's *Noches lúgubres*,[64] and certainly more markedly revolutionary than either of these in the poem 'En alabanza de un carpintero llamado Alfonso'. Hermosilla was surprised that in spite of its 'ideas demasiado republicanas' this poem passed the censorship in 1816. It begins by attacking the corrupt moral values of courts and magnates, and asserting that justice and reason can only be found in the 'congojosa choza del infeliz',

> desde que fiero,
> ayugando al humano,
> de la igualdad triunfo el primer tirano.[65]

Equality is the law of nature and those who are rich and ignore their duty towards their fellow-men ought to be destroyed:

> Disipad, destruid, oh colosales
> monstruos de la fortuna las riquezas
> en la perversidad y torpe olvido
> de la santa razón: criad, brutales
> en nueva iniquidad, nuevas grandezas
> y nueva destrucción: y el duro oído
> a la piedad negando,
> que Alfonso expire, en hambre desmayando.[66]

It is noticeable, however, that in this passage the overthrow of the unjust order by Fortune is not thought to bring equity, and Cienfuegos, although more outspoken and vehement on matters of social justice and equality, reflects not the desire for a change of system so much as a sharpened sense of obligation and charity within the existing system. This is precisely the position of Jovellanos at the end of his 'Sátira segunda a Arnesto', in a set of lines which were not published when the poem first came out in *El Censor* in 1787.[67] The value-system of the nobility is seen as something which may well lead to revolution. But the state of anarchy which would follow is 'infame', and the people's seizing of power usurpation:

> Faltó el apoyo de las leyes. Todo
> se precipita: el más humilde cieno
> fermenta, y brota espíritus altivos,
> que hasta los tronos del Olimpo se alzan.
> ¿Que importa? Venga denodada, venga
> la humilde plebe en usurpación y usurpe
> lustre, nobleza, títulos y honores.

4 * *

Sea todo infame behetría: no haya
clases ni estados. Si la virtud sola
les puede ser antemural y escudo,
todo sin ella acabe y se confunda.[68]

The form of Cienfuegos's poems is consistent with this view. 'En
alabanza de un carpintero', for example, has a conventional *canción*
stanza structure of eight lines (ABCABCdD) with very few irregulari-
ties. The same precision of form is characteristic of his other poems
too. At the same time the rhetorical tone of Cienfuegos seems a new
development, as does the range of his imagination. If Meléndez's
imagination is stimulated by what he feels through his senses, Cienfuegos's is also awakened by what he sees in his mind's eye. At the
end of 'La primavera' he imagines a Swiss landscape, and although
his imaginings deceive him—a common Enlightenment topic—they
are nevertheless described as 'sueños *amados* de la imaginación'.[69]
This interest in the imagination is consistent with the new interests in
theories of the Sublime in Spain as elsewhere in Europe in the late
eighteenth century.[70] Indeed, a work entitled *Reflexiones sobre la
Poesía* published in Madrid in 1787 by an anonymous writer calling
himself N. Philoaletheias picked on the then unknown Cienfuegos as
one of the few poets in Spain capable of writing poetry of imagination
rather than analysis.[71] For 'Philoaletheias', imaginative poetry was not
only the sole true type of poetry but also the only type of poetry
possible for the free man in an age which no longer believed in the
superstitions of earlier times. The lines of Cienfuegos quoted by
'Philoaletheias'—'¿Quién a la luna plateada ha hecho/lucir en el
silencio oscuramente?'[72]—are from a poem of his which has not
survived. But the second line is rich in sense material and the oxymoron 'lucir oscuramente' hints at the mystery surrounding the nature
of the deity which is characteristic of the Enlightenment. The rhetorical question too as a reflection of a certain intensity of emotion is
often used by Cienfuegos, as is the exclamation and the repetition of
single words or phrases for dramatic effect.[73]

Cienfuegos was not entirely pleased to have lines which did not
scan well mentioned in the book. He argued in a letter to the *Diario
de Madrid* on 4 November 1787, that Philoaletheias's assertion that
poetry should be wholly a product of the imagination was tantamount
to saying that 'a delirious person must be the greatest poet'. Poetry

for Cienfuegos, as art for Goya, required a combination of reason and imagination.

The ideas and sensual qualities of Cienfuegos's kind of poetry did not go unchallenged. In 1793, Padre Isidoro Pérez de Celis published the first part of a long poem entitled *Filosofía de las costumbres* whose avowed aim was to combat 'the pernicious abuse which those who call themselves Philosophers have recently made of Reason and Poetry with the object of encouraging profligacy'. Pérez de Celis upheld the Church, the monarchy, and parental authority. To stylistic conservatives, Cienfuegos's poetry seemed an undesirable, almost Gongoristic, development. On the other hand, some thought it brought an injection of native passion into eighteenth-century Spanish poetry, which Forner, for instance, felt had been lost as a result of the imitation and translation of French originals.[74] A vein of patriotism certainly affected the development of poetry at the end of the century. The Neo-classics had believed that it was their patriotic duty to raise Spanish literature to the level of other European literatures by accepting the Classical criteria which ruled the rest of Europe. Exacerbated by the continued disregard for Spanish literature expressed by foreigners at the end of the century, Spaniards now made an attempt to revive specifically Spanish forms. The admiration for Luis de León expressed by Salamanca poets and that for Herrera expressed by Cienfuegos fit within the Neo-classical framework.[75] But there was little Neo-classic about the enthusiasm for the *romancero* and the popular *seguidillas* which developed in the early nineteenth century.

Patriotism could also be reflected in theme as well as form. The poetry of the Peninsular War period is an obvious case in point, though many poets, Juan Bautista Arriaza (1770-1837) for instance, attacked France in the sublime style learned from France as well as from England. Neo-classic forms died hard. They lived on in fact through most of the nineteenth century.[76] Independent poetic forms, encouraged no doubt by a progressive loss of confidence in the political hierarchy as a result of the weakness of Charles IV as well as the French Revolution, developed slowly.

The beginning of a liberation in form as well as in content can perhaps be most clearly seen in Quintana. Quintana shared Cienfuegos's aesthetic principles as well as his political opinions. In dedicating his *Poesías* to his dead friend in 1813, Quintana claimed that he had learned from Cienfuegos

> a no hacer de la literatura un instrumento de opresión y de servidumbre; a no degradar jamás ni con la adulación ni con la sátira la noble profesión de escribir; a manejar y respetar la poesía como un don que el cielo dispensa a los hombres para que se perfeccionen y se amen, y no para que se destrocen y corrompan.

War, injustice, religious and political tyranny on the one hand; peace, liberty, patriotism, a sense of society, virtue, and beauty on the other. These are Quintana's themes. His poetry struck his contemporaries as being a strange mixture. The manner of its expression is at root traditional: the *canción* and the *silva* of the sixteenth century, the *romance*. Yet Quintana is much more prepared to adapt these forms and modify them than previous poets had been. Take the poem to 'Juan de Padilla', for instance, written in May 1797. It is in hendecasyllables and heptasyllables, and the stanzas are reasonably uniform, ranging in length between fourteen and twelve lines, with some of three or four lines more. The basic pattern would seem to be that of the *silva*, but Quintana neither wholly preserves nor abandons the rhyme scheme. There is an incipient liberation from conventions here.[77]

Yet in many respects Quintana and his contemporaries could not break with the kind of society in which they had grown up, nor with its values. Enslavement and tyranny offended them. Paternalism, however, was acceptable. The lesson Quintana saw in the duquesa de Alba's adoption of a negro baby (in the poem 'A una negrita') was that the establishment did not always ignore the individual's need for freedom, and could, in a way, allow it. The duquesa was admired for her motherly approach, just as earlier Neo-classics admired Charles III for being the father of his people.

Individual virtue, the senses of the individual, the freedom of the individual, these are what mattered to Quintana and his contemporaries. They were rather more independent of society's values than the poets of the beginning of the eighteenth century, but new forms and attitudes did not suddenly appear. Sánchez Barbero's (1764-1819) satire on the Inquisition is couched in the form of a parody of Garcilaso's first eclogue;[78] Cristóbal de Beña's and Ramón de Valvidares y Longo's attacks on tyranny and bad government are cast in the framework of the fable, a traditional European form which Iriarte had used in his *Fábulas literarias* to express the literary ideals so often associated with absolutist regimes, and whose mixture of delight and morality seems particularly Neo-classical. Pablo de Jérica (1781-1831) also used the fable, to such good political effect that the prologue to the Bordeaux 1831 edition of his poems could declare that 'los liberales, especialmente los jóvenes, las estiman; y los serviles, sobre todo los fanáticos, las detestan'.

What certainly happens in the early years of the nineteenth century is that poetry shows an ever-increasing concern for imaginative force rather than for organisation. In the note which precedes Arriaza's *Fragmentos de la Silvia*, the poet speaks of the 'imposibilidad que hay siempre de suplir con frías añadiduras el primer ardor de la imaginación que inspire los primeros versos'.[79] Similarly, when the poems of Padre Bogiero (1752-1809) were compared with the paintings of Goya by 'D.L.G.P.' who published the former's *Poesías* in Madrid in 1817, he singled out for praise in both artists 'invención, imaginación, expresión feliz, novedad, singularidad y aquel no sé qué por el cual los talentos originales no se parecen sino a sí mismos'.[80] Of these, only 'expresión feliz', felicity of expression, fits readily into normal Neo-classical categories. The other good points seem rather to derive from Longinus, whose *Treatise on the sublime* Bogiero himself translated into Spanish.

Yet praise for originality is still rare in the early years of the nineteenth century.[81] The acceptance of sweeping changes in art forms had to wait for further and deeper changes in Spanish society.

NOTES

1. This phrase of Luzán occurs in Book I, chapter 9 of the *Poética* (ed. L. de Filippo, Barcelona, 1956, I, 71). Similar points are made and Horace's 'utile dulci' quoted in Book I, chapters 5 and 6 (ibid., 55 *et seq.*).

2. 'Todas las artes, como es razón, están subordinadas a la política, cuyo objeto es el bien público, y la que más coopera a la política es la moral, cuyos preceptos ordenan las costumbres y dirigen los ánimos a la bienaventuranza eterna y temporal' (*Poética*, ed. cit., I, 71). Similar views are expressed when Luzán speaks about the Homeric poems in chapter 4.

3. Nigel Glendinning, 'La fortuna de Góngora en el siglo XVIII', 327.

4. *Soledad Tercera siguiendo las dos que dexó escritas el príncipe de los poetas líricos de España D. Luis de Góngora ... compuesta por Don Joseph de León y Mansilla* (Córdoba, 1718), Al Lector.

5. *BAE*, 61 (Madrid, 1869), p. 6b.

6. Leopoldo Augusto Cueto, 'Bosquejo histórico-crítico de la poesía castellana en el siglo XVIII', *BAE*, 61, pp. lxxxix *et seq.*

7. ibid., pp. 14-15.

8. *Polifemo*, ll. 309-12.

9. *Polifemo*, ll. 213-16. See commentary by Dámaso Alonso, in *Góngora y el Polifemo*, 4th ed. (Madrid, 1961), II, 156-7.

10. He also affirms his desire to avoid 'el estilo sino rústico, ordinario' and follows Góngora in wishing his works to be 'sólo estudio de la erudición más elevada'.

11. For biographical information about Porcel, see E. Orozco, 'Porcel y el barroquismo literario del siglo XVIII', *CCF*, 21 (1968), 20-36.

12. *BAE*, 61, p. 140 a/b.

13. Garcilaso de la Vega, *Poesías castellanas completas*, ed. E. L. Rivers (Madrid, 1969), pp. 205-6.

14. *BAE*, 61, p. 141 b.

15. See Dámaso Alonso, op. cit., I, 196 *et seq.*

16. Porcel uses the *estribillo* 'Oh, bienaventurado/Quien de ti no se fía' at the beginning and end of a series of six parallel stanzas of varying length (13, 12, 6, 8, 8, and 8 lines respectively) reminiscent of the more regular *Soledades*, I, ll. 94-135.

17. Cf. *BAE*, 61, pp. 143 a and 149 a; 146 b and 152 a.

18. *BAE*, 61, pp. 26, 34, 44, 47, etc. ('Carta pastoril a un condiscípulo', 'Envió un regalo de perniles y chorizos al conde de Águila', 'Décimas improvisadas en una tertulia', 'Enviando cuatro búcaros en el de su cumpleaños a una señora recién vestida de beata', 'Definición del chichisveo, escrita por obedecer a una dama', etc.).

19. See Alcalá Galiano's criticism of his supposedly Gongorine style in *BAE*, 61, p. 21.

20. *Diario de los literatos de España*, IV.2 (Madrid, 1738), 349.

21. N. Glendinning, 'La fortuna de Góngora . . .', 336.

22. *Orígenes de la poesía castellana* (Málaga, 1754)—'Conclusión de este escrito'.

23. On the influence of the Jesuits see Nigel Glendinning, 'Cartas inéditas de Cadalso a un Padre Jesuita en inglés, francés, español y latín', *BBMP*, XLII (1966), 97-8. For Classical precepts in the schools, see above, pp. 24-5.

24. Nicolás Fernández de Moratín, *El Poeta* (Madrid, 1764), pp. 33 *et seq.*, Anacreóntica v.

25. ibid., p. 35; *BAE*, 2, p. 1.

26. For information about the economic background of the Esquilache riots, see C. Eguía Ruiz, *Los jesuitas y el Motín de Esquilache* (Madrid, 1947), pp. 15 *et seq.*

27. *BAE*, 2, p. 32 a.

28. ibid., p. 53 b.

29. ibid., p. 65 b ('Feijoo, mi gran Feijoo, las pirineas/cumbres pasar los hizo, y ha mostrado/El rumbo a las solidísimas ideas').

30. ibid., p. 63 b.

31. For Feijoo's relatively favourable consideration of Copernican theory see I. L. McClelland, *Benito Jerónimo Feijoo* (New York, 1969), pp. 138-9. Luzán's view is embodied in his *Juicio de París*. After matter about atomic and corpuscular theories and gravitation he speaks of the sun in the following

terms: 'La tierra inmóvil su gran curso admira,/O bien voluble en torno a Febo gira' (*BAE*, 61, p. 114 a). It should be remembered that as late as 1774, the censor of a work entitled *Los elementos de todas las ciencias* could assert of Copernican theory that 'aunque es cierto que es el [sistema] que se sigue generalmente, no se tiene por demostrado todavía, y mientras esto no se verifique, bastará admitirle como una hipótesi' (see Serrano y Sanz, 'El Consejo de Castilla y la censura de los libros en el siglo XVIII', *RABM*, XVI, 1907, 108).

32. See Advertencia to *Arte de las Putas. Poema. Lo escribió Nicolás Fernández de Moratín* (Madrid, 1898).

33. ibid., p. 16.

34. 'El arte de verter la sangre humana/con la espada fatal es aprendido/ de Príncipes y grandes . . . Son much más leves/mis delitos: no incito asolamientos,/destrucciones ni muertes horrorosas,/sólo facilitar las deleitosas/complacencias de amor . . .' (ed. cit., pp. 20-1).

35. See Nigel Glendinning, *Vida y obra de Cadalso* (Madrid, 1962), p. 39. The discussion no doubt was sparked off by a common interest in Villegas, and there was useful material in Luzán's *Poética*, Book II, chapter 22 ('Del metro de los versos vulgares').

36. For Cadalso's banishment, see N. Glendinning, *Vida y obra de Cadalso*, pp. 122-5; and for García de la Huerta's *RL*, fascs. 27-8 (1958), pp. 3-23. Moratín's banishment is undocumented, but there is certainly evidence of a separation from society which seemed to him comparable to exile, yet not merely the result of an unfortunate love affair in his *romance* 'A un amigo desde San Ildefonso' (*BAE*, 2, p. 18 a/b).

37. Josef Vázquez, *Ocios de mi juventud* (Madrid, 1773), f A 2 r/v.

38. See Luzán's *Poética* (Barcelona, 1956), I, 93.

39. I do not know of any clear precedents for Cadalso's arrangement. Common patterns were arrangements by verse forms, by muses, or by mixture for variety's sake. Herrera's poems sometimes, however, seem arranged to move from the particular to the general in their treatment of themes, and the Licenciado Isidro Flórez de Laviada implied that the whole of the conde de Rebolledo's *Ocios* could have a construction put upon it, when he maintained that the first part 'se reduce a un honesto *arte amandi* y erudito *remedio amoris*' (see Rebolledo, *Obras*, Madrid, 1778, Tomo I, Parte Primera).

40. *La Serafina* (Saragossa, 1959), p. 157.

41. *BAE*, 61, p. 269 c.

42. See Vicente de los Ríos, *Memorias de la vida y escritos de Villegas*, in Vol. I of the 2nd Sancha edition of *Las eróticas* (Madrid, 1797), § 39.

43. See Nigel Glendinning, 'Influencia de la literatura inglesa en España en el siglo XVIII', 71 *et seq*.

44. Alban Forcione, 'Meléndez Valdés and the "Essay on Man"', *HR*, XXXIV (1966), 291-306.

45. See A. O. Lovejoy, *The Great Chain of Being, a study of the history of an idea* (Cambridge, Mass., 1961). A French writer in the great chain tradition who was well known in Spain was Louis Racine, whose poem *La religion* was translated by Antonio Ranza Romanillos and published in Madrid in 1786.

46. *Fábulas literarias*, No. 49.

47. *Discurso* III, 'Orden del universo y cadena admirable de sus seres' in *Poesías* (Valladolid, 1797), III, 280.

48. 'La despedida del anciano', *El Censor*, No. 154, 24 May 1787.

49. *Poesías*, III, 249–51.

50. ibid., I, iv.

51. ed. cit., p. 113.

52. See N. Glendinning, 'Influencia de la literatura inglesa en España en el siglo XVIII', 87–8.

53. See W. E. Colford, *Juan Meléndez Valdés. A Study in the Transition from Neo-classicism to Romanticism in Spanish Poetry* (New York, Hispanic Institute, 1942), pp. 192 *et seq.* See also César Real de la Riva, 'La escuela poética salmantina del siglo XVIII', *BBMP*, XXIV (1948), 32–64. An important further source of much Nature poetry at the period was Gessner, on whose influence in Spain cf. J. L. Cano in *RLC*, XXXV (1961), 40–60.

54. *BAE*, 61, p. 465 a/b.

55. See *Noches lúgubres*, ed. N. Glendinning, p. 33.

56. See Góngora, *Obras completas*, ed. Juan and Isabel Millé y Giménez (Madrid, 1943), p. 493, No. 387—'espejos claros de cristal luciente'. 'Cristal' for water is a commonplace in the *Soledades* and the *Polifemo*, so is the adjective 'luciente', but I have not found the two together. 'Jaspe luciente' occurs in the *Panegírico al duque de Lerma* for water (l. 215), and it seems that Góngora only uses 'luciente' when the object qualified is a source of strong light. In the instance quoted the moon is reflected in water. Possibly the phrase is used more precisely by Góngora than by Iglesias.

57. *BAE*, 61, p. 465 a.

58. Meléndez Valdés, *Poesías*, ed. Pedro Salinas (Madrid, CC, 1925), p. 230.

59. ibid, p. 269.

60. ibid., p. 271.

61. This is not always the case in Meléndez. He often writes poems which begin with generalisations and move to particular (even personal or apparently personal) applications, as in *Romance* XXIX 'La mañana', for example. He also uses nature conventionally to symbolise such general ideas as the passage of time. But even in poems of this latter kind he often puts in an observer (sometimes a fictional one), and his fondness for the senses is also borne out by his interest in images. Alterations and revisions made to many of his poems show this interest in images, often for their own sake—i.e. their sense appeal. In a later version of a poem he often merely adds additional images, in no way changing the sense of the poem as a whole.

62. Cienfuegos, *Poesías*, ed. J. L. Cano (Madrid, CCa., 1969), p. 118.

63. ibid., p. 12.

64. For a study of the topic of friendship at this period, see J. L. Cano, 'Cienfuegos y la amistad', *Clavileño*, 34 (1955), 35–40.

65. *Poesías*, ed. cit., p. 161, ll. 22-4.

66. ibid., p. 166, ll. 224-31.

67. See Jovellanos, *Poesías*, ed. José Caso González (Oviedo, 1962), pp. 241 *et seq.*

68. ibid., p. 253.

69. Cienfuegos, *Poesías*, ed. cit., p. 110, ll. 270–1.

70. See above, pp. 23–5. Also Menéndez y Pelayo, *Historia de las ideas estéticas en España*, in *Obras completas* (Santander, 1947), III, 178 *et seq.*

71. See J. L. Cano, 'Una "Poética" desconocida del XVIII. Las "Re-

flexiones sobre la poesía" de N. Philoaletheias (1787)', *BH*, LXIII, No. 1–2 (1961), 86.

72. ibid.

73. '¡Oh salve, salve soledad querida[!]' (*Poesías*, ed. cit., p. 111); further examples are 'otoño, otoño' (p. 112); 'copa, copa' and 'luego, luego' (p. 112); 'en vano, en vano' (p. 114). Other instances on pp. 117, 118, 119, and 121, etc.

74. Forner criticised the 'ridícula y servil imitación del Diálogo ultramontano' in the theatre in his *Colección de pensamientos filosóficos, sentencias y dichos grandes de los más célebres poetas dramáticos españoles* (Madrid, 1786), I, viii.

75. Cienfuegos, *Poesías*, ed. cit., pp. 12-13 (J. L. Cano's introduction).

76. It is worth recalling that Rubén Darío was still attacking Neo-classic ideas (and Gómez Hermosilla, their chief proponent in the 1820s) in his story *El rey burgués* in *Azul* . . . (1888).

77. For a study of Quintana's use of *silva* see Albert Dérozier, *Manuel Josef Quintana et la naissance du libéralisme en Espagne* (*Annales littéraires de l'université de Besançon*, 95, Paris, 1968), pp. 168 *et seq.* For a critical view see Antonio Alcalá Galiano, *Literatura española siglo XIX*, translated Vicente Llorens (Madrid, 1969), p. 87.

78. *Ensayos satíricos en verso y prosa por el Licenciado Machuca* (Madrid, 1820), 'La muerte de la Inquisición. Egloga sepulcral. Flamesio, Rancinoso', pp. 46-58.

79. *Ensayos poéticos de D. Juan Bautista de Arriaza* (Palma, 1811), p. 55.

80. ibid., p. xi. See also A. Rodríguez-Moñino, 'Goya y Gallardo: noticias de su amistad' in *Relieves de erudición* (Valencia, 1959), p. 339.

81. There is a sharp distinction between 'imitación servil y pedestre' and praise of intelligent imitation. See Rafael José Crespo's prologue to his *Fábulas morales y literarias* (Saragossa, 1820), p. 7. Crespo defends himself against possible criticism for lack of originality. The continuance of basically Neo-classical criteria at the same period is particularly marked in Alberto Lista, who commented adversely, like José Joaquín de Mora, on Schlegel's theories when they first began to be read in Spain. See his 'Reflexiones sobre la dramática española en los siglos XVI y XVII' (*El Censor*, No. 38, 21 de abril de 1821) and Hans Juretschke, *Vida, obra y pensamiento de Alberto Lista* (Madrid, 1951).

Chapter 4

EIGHTEENTH-CENTURY DRAMA

MOST EARLY EIGHTEENTH-CENTURY THEATRE in Spain continues seventeenth-century formulas and practices as surely as early eighteenth-century poetry persists in the traditions of the age of Góngora. The frequent publication and performance of plays by Calderón in the eighteenth century is clearly an important factor, both reflecting and stimulating the continuance of the tradition. There is no break in the performance of Golden Age plays between 1700 and 1808, although these were often radically altered to suit the taste of the times.[1] Court taste changed too, and Philip V's preference for the Italian opera no doubt affected the Spanish theatre in the 1720s and 30s,[2] as did the marqués de Grimaldi's and the conde de Aranda's support for French Neo-classic plays at Court in the late 1760s.[3] Popular taste for spectacle rather than ideas, on the other hand, meant that both the Neo-classic works of the 1770s and 80s and the Golden Age works put on at the same period often played to minority audiences, as ticket sales for Madrid theatres show.[4] The less educated members of the public probably did not really enjoy unspectacular Golden Age plays any more than their English contemporaries took pleasure in watching Shakespeare, as Leandro Fernández de Moratín observed. What the general public really wanted in the 1750s, according to Montiano y Luyando, was 'cuatro chistes de Prado, Puerta del Sol, Lavapiés o Barquillo, y . . . la vistosa disposición de tramoyas y bastidores'.[5] A producer in the 1770s maintained that the most suitable plays for performance were those which could provide for the climactic entry of a triumphal car. Ramón de la Cruz in his *El deseo de seguidillas* (1769) implied that the poorer theatregoers mainly judged plays by their 'tramoyas', but also liked *sainetes* and song-and-dance routines; and in Valladolid in 1788 the 'corrupt and jaded palates' of the average theatregoer still craved scenic effects like 'transportines de nieve, murallas undosas, [y] monstruosas hidras de plata'.[6]

Several of the dramatists who dominated the early years of the century have already been discussed in an earlier volume, and only Cañizares (1676-1750) and Antonio de Zamora (1660?-1728) need be mentioned here. Their works were first performed at the Madrid theatres (Cruz and Príncipe) and in the Retiro Palace from the late 1690s in the case of Zamora and from 1704 to 1727 in the case of Cañizares, although some of the latter's works were put on for the first time as late as 1742. Both knew how to make their plays spectacular as well as moral. Paul Mérimée's conclusions about these dramatists in his unpublished thesis *La littérature dramatique espagnole dans la première moitié du XVIIIe siècle* (Toulouse, 1955) point to some development in their work in relation to Calderón: a tendency in Zamora towards a more regular framework, but with a more complicated intrigue and a straining for picturesque and spectacular effect; and an evolution towards a semi-burlesque satire of social behaviour from 1712 onwards. So far as versification is concerned, Julius A. Molinaro and W. T. McCready's analysis of Cañizares's *zarzuela Angélica y Medoro* suggests that there may have been some moves at this period towards a new variety after the tendency towards simplification in the late seventeenth century.[7] Three changes of verse form in an act was normally the minimum and eight a maximum—mostly switches from *romance* to *redondillas*, as was common practice at the end of the seventeenth century.[8] But other verse forms were used and in a number of plays music was introduced, adding richness of texture and variety.

Generally speaking, these dramatists used versification and music more for variety's sake than because they added to the meaning of the play. And this fact, together with the criticism of the Spanish theatre common outside Spain, no doubt invited the reassessment of the traditions Zamora and Cañizares had inherited, as we find in Luzán's *Poética* (1737). Luzán was worried, as seventeenth-century moralists had been, about the dangers of representing immoral situations on the stage. He also felt that there was a lack of 'estudio y arte' in Lope and Calderón, although he admired the latter's ability to keep his audience gripped.

But when some eighteenth-century followers of Calderón were gripping audiences almost solely by spectacle, it is easy to understand the misgivings of serious-minded critics in Spain. In a play published in 1740 about the life of Cardinal Cisneros, which Cadalso later mocked in the *Suplemento a los Eruditos a la violeta*,[9] there are clouds with rain, a real donkey, and indications that Fray Francisco should levitate, fly rapidly on a rope across the stalls up to the balconies on the left-hand side, and appear in the air on a white horse, 'dando tornos . . . y con el cordón echando a los moros que están en la muralla'.[10]

Luzán's concern for public morality, reason, and the ordered society is very typical of his generation, and to be expected at a period when most people could still remember the divided Spain of the early years of the century and the War of the Spanish Succession. The theatre was felt by Luzán and others to be an ideal instrument for social and moral reform, and to make the best use of it meant a proper balance of 'utility and delight'. As Luzán wrote, 'Un poema épico, una tragedia, o una comedia, en quien ni a la utilidad sazone el deleite, ni al deleite temple y modere la utilidad, o serán infructuosas por lo que les falta, o nocivos por lo que les sobra'.[11]

The first eighteenth-century attempts to produce tragedies—a genre which foreigners believed Spanish dramatists to be incapable of writing[12]—were made by Luzán's friend Montiano y Luyando (1697-1764) in the early 1750s, and it is instructive to compare his *Virginia* and *Ataulpho* with seventeenth-century Spanish plays. The superficial concern for unities of time, place, and action need not detain us, but his two plays' structure, meaning, and dramatic techniques are worth considering.

Ataulpho is the simpler of the two. The forces of good and evil are ranged against one another from the first act: on the one hand are Placidia, the Roman wife of Ataulpho, Gothic King of Spain, and the King himself, Prince Valia, and a Roman ambassador, Constancio; on the other, Rosamunda, greedy for power and jealous of Placidia, allied with the ambitious Sigerico and Vernulpho. The dramatic interest lies in the discovery by Ataulpho and Placidia of the various plans laid against them. There are some psychologically effective moments, like Scene vi of Act III, in which Placidia pretends to believe in Rosamunda's alleged motives, and then tries to force from her an admission of the truth she already knows. Motives and values are of the essence in this play, and the denouement brings the tragic death of the good Ataulpho. But there is more at stake here than just morality, important though that is. Equally important is the conflict between the civilised, peace-loving, controlled society for which Ataulpho, Placidia, and Valia stand, and the warlike, barbarous, and divisive society represented by the personal ambitions and uncontrolled passions of Sigerico, Rosamunda, and Vernulpho. Since the setting is Spanish it is hard not to see this as a social as well as a moral object lesson.

Virginia is set in Rome and concerns the sexual designs, political ambitions, and tyranny of Apio Claudio, a decemvir, who lusts after Virginia, promised to Lucio Icilio. Claudio's desire to be an absolute ruler politically is echoed by his readiness to usurp her love. In the last act, Lucio Virginio, Virginia's father, kills his daughter to save her from dishonour; later we are told that the tyrant himself has died, killed by his own hand when about to be attacked by Icilio. The play has a double plot, and Montiano tends to deal with the two sides, love and politics, act and act about. Technically, therefore, the structure of the play is rather clumsy and unsubtle, and does not bear comparison with Lope's *Fuenteovejuna*, for example, which joins the themes of political and amorous tyranny much more ingeniously. The concern with feelings and attitudes rather than with action, the unchanging verse-structure (unrhymed hendecasyllables), and the Classical setting clearly owe something to Montiano's interest in the French seventeenth-century theatre, though the particular orientation towards political as well as personal morality seems an eighteenth-century development comparable with Voltaire's theatre in France.[13]

In this respect Montiano seems to have taken Luzán very much to heart. Luzán is very specific about the lessons for courtiers and princes to be found in the theatre. 'No es menor la utilidad que produce la tragedia',[14] he writes,

en quien los Príncipes pueden aprender a moderar su ambición, su ira, y otras pasiones, con los ejemplos que allí se representan de Príncipes caídos de una suma felicidad a una extrema miseria; cuyo escarmiento les acuerda la inconstancia de las cosas humanas, y los previene y fortalece contra los reveses de la fortuna. Además de esto el Poeta puede y debe pintar en la Tragedia las costumbres y los artificios de los cortesanos aduladores y ambiciosos ... todo lo cual puede ser una escuela provechosísima, que enseña a conocer

lo que es corte, y lo que son cortesanos, y a descifrar los dobleces
de la fina política, y de ese monstruo que llaman razón de estado.

Much of this could perhaps have been said of seventeenth-century
Spanish plays with equal validity. But Luzán's conception of tragedy
differs in one major respect: the 'extrema miseria' to which a prince
may finally be brought is death itself. This conclusion was repugnant
to seventeenth-century Spanish practice,[15] which demanded recogni-
tion of the divine and the social orders, reconciliation where possible,
and punishment where necessary; but not, as a rule, the death of a
ruler, whether innocent or guilty.

Montiano's use of the death of innocent characters in both his
tragedies—Virginia herself in the one and Ataulpho in the other—
suggests that he was striving for a strong emotional effect in his plays
as well as political and moral points. The search for emotional
intensity is borne out by the detail of these tragedies as well as by
their plots and situations, further illustrating the author's preoccupation with human attitudes and values. Placidia's first speech in
Scene v, Act III of *Ataulpho* is a good example of the use of
repetition to create tension; elsewhere, broken speeches and tears (as
in Act IV, Scene vi) seek to project the conflicts and doubts in
emotional human terms.

But these points pale into insignificance beside the political overtones. Ataulpho himself not only supports peace and good relations
with other states, but seems also to advocate an enlightened despotism: freedom and justice within a firmly controlled state,
threatened by the independent ambitions of aristocrats. In fact,
Ataulpho dramatises the duties of the noble class, with Valia as a
good example and Sigerico and Vernulpho as bad ones. The same
is true of *Virginia*, which politically is more audacious, in that it
depicts good nobles rising against an unjust tyrant when no other
course remains open to them.

In view of the subjects of these plays it is perhaps not surprising
that they were never performed. It would be interesting to know more
about the range of political as well as literary topics discussed in
Montiano's circle, particularly since one of his closest friends, the
marqués de Valdeflores, was one of those suspected of political
involvement in the Esquilache riots in the 1760s.[16]

Amongst Montiano's protégés was Nicolás Fernández de Moratín, who produced four plays in the 1760s and early 1770s. The earliest was the comedy *La Petimetra* (1762), very traditional in its form and dramatic structure.[17] Two young ladies and their maid, two young gentlemen and their manservant, and the ladies' guardian make up the cast. One young man is in love with Jerónima before the action begins, and when the other also falls in love with her, it is not hard to predict the pattern of the story. Both men later switch their attentions to the other lady, María; one because she has a dowry, and the other because he realises that she is more sensible and also that he has been in love with her before. The play is concerned with the contrasting standards of the four central characters, two of whom (María and Félix) uphold worthwhile values while the other two judge everything by appearances. A good deal of hiding in closets and under tables goes on in a conventional way, and there are stylised parallel speeches from Félix and Damián in Scenes xii and xv of Act II. The only unusual feature is the observance of the unities of time, place, and action. The limited use of verse forms is not unusual in the seventeenth- and early eighteenth-century theatre. *Redondillas* and *romance* are used alternately throughout. Also, contrary to seventeenth-century practice, Moratín makes love and honour less a question of morality than of reason. Love is natural, and the seventeenth-century approach here gives way to that of the Enlightenment.

Infinitely more interesting, however, are Moratín's tragedies, whose subjects are drawn from Roman and Spanish history: *Lucrecia,* like Montiano's *Virginia,* is set in Rome, *Guzmán el Bueno* and *Hormesinda* in Spain during the period of struggle against the Moors. In the latter there are obvious nationalistic overtones, particularly appropriate, no doubt, for the unsettled Madrid society of the Post-Esquilache riot period. The basic subject of *Hormesinda* is the dangerous force of the passions, but there is an interesting concern for the influence of education and environment on the individual's morality and also a political relevance in the criticism of absolute power. Munuza believes in this, but Fernández, in Scene vi of Act IV, attacks Spaniards who respect tyrants as well as kings. Trasmundo's rejoinder that such things could not exist in Spain— 'más es padre que rey un rey de España'[18]—no doubt pleased the censors.

In *Hormesinda,* as in *La Petimetra,* the characters are rather black and white, but their blackness and whiteness is presented as a result of their nurture rather than nature. Hormesinda, for instance, speaks of the moral force of her unbringing in Act IV, Scene i, while Munuza declares he has been brought up on treachery in Scene iii of the same act. The possible impact of the pleasure-loving environment of Córdoba on character is mentioned in Act II, Scene iv. Elsewhere in the play this view is expanded into the kind of discussion about religion and society that was common in the eighteenth century. Differences of religion do not necessarily mean differences of moral standards. As Pelayo says to Fernández:

> no los ritos,
> No la contraria religión al hombre
> Con el otro hombre a ser infiel obliga,
> Ni impide que la ley cada cual siga
> Que halló en su educación o su destino
> (Arcano que venero, y no examino),
> Para que el pecho, a quien razón gobierna,
> Sensible a la amistad, al fin humano
> Corresponda, a pesar del dogma vano.[19]

The importance that Moratín here gives to moral standards rather than to religious dogma is still more striking in his *Lucrecia*, where naturally the morally good characters are not Christian. The suicide ending is in line with Stoic doctrine, following a common eighteenth-century dramatic practice with an obvious paradigm in Addison's *Cato*. *Lucrecia* is even more outspoken than *Hormesinda* in its condemnation of absolutism. Tarquino believes that his position gives him the right to do as he likes, and his court flatterer Mevio declares in Act I, Scene v:

> Al príncipe, señor, lícito es todo
> Cuanto gustare.[20]

But Tarquino's seduction of Lucrecia, which is shown as moral treachery and as a counterpart to the political treachery which he has practised in the past (Act II, Scene i), leads to the overthrow of tyranny and the re-establishment of liberty and good government. Perhaps Moratín had to be slightly more cautious in discussing these ideas after the Esquilache riotings in 1766.[21] The later play,

Hormesinda, may reflect the restraints imposed on writers by the government at that period.

More limited in its range is Moratín's third tragedy, *Guzmán el Bueno,* another essay in patriotism, with a central Cornelian tension between duty towards Spain and love for son and family. Heroic virtue and self-discipline are contrasted with passion and impetuosity in a well-organised structure of suspense. The political aspects of the work are of negligible interest, however, and the religious attitudes expressed in the play are mostly traditional and orthodox, although Guzmán does suggest that 'la virtud en todas religiones/tiene lugar'[22] in Act II, Scene viii. There is a relapse into the association of heroic virtue with noble birth.

So far as dramatic techniques are concerned, Moratín has a tauter sense of structure than Montiano. Furthermore, he has a much more sensitive ear than his mentor and exploits sound effects to the full. His tragedies make extensive use of rhyming hendecasyllabic couplets, but Moratín does not hesitate to intersperse his couplets with lines that do not rhyme, so that there is no lack of freedom for the poet within the system, and no sense that meaning has been distorted to preserve the pattern of rhyme. Following the precept of Luzán[23] and the practice of Montiano, Moratín expresses the salient ideas of his plays in aphoristic form, and makes a good deal of broken speeches and exclamations to convey emotion; there are also occasional effective instances of alliteration.

Less lively and flexible from certain points of view is Cadalso's *Don Sancho García,* produced early in 1771, very shortly after Moratín's *Hormesinda.* Cadalso uses rhyming couplets throughout, and also keeps rigidly to the unities. Like earlier Neo-classical playwrights he assures the verisimilitude of his tragedy by choosing a historical subject, and a plot which gives rise to tension within a family group, as recommended for tragedy by Aristotle.[24] In the Condesa too he creates a tragic character in the Classical mould; neither wholly good nor bad, but falling on account of a moral flaw. The metre is less flexible and the Neo-classic principles are applied more rigorously than in the case of Moratín (though the political and religious ideas involved are more progressive). Although the setting is the Moorish-Christian struggle, there is one Moor, Alek, whose moral values are as impeccable as those of any Christian in the play. And evil passions sway the Christian Condesa as violently as they do the Moorish Prince Almanzor, although their respective passions are different: hers being love, while his is political ambition.

In form, Cadalso's play works towards the Classical double catastrophe: the fall of the bad and the salvation of the good. In spite of the careful Classical techniques, the play is unsatisfying dramatically. Suspense is sustained throughout as to whether or not the Condesa will accede to the request of her lover Almanzor and kill her son, Don Sancho García. But the range of tensions is rather narrow for a five-act play.

In Cadalso, as in Moratín and Montiano, the concern with the duties of nobles and their right to criticise the king is of paramount importance. The noble's right to advise the sovereign against a course of action he believes to be wrong or unjust is once again stated (through Alek), and the duties of nobles are set out in a long speech from Sancho García's mentor, Don Gonzalo. This speech was singled out for praise by Sempere y Guarinos in the article on Cadalso in his *Ensayo de una biblioteca española de los mejores escritores del reinado de Carlo III*.[25] If the moral lessons of the play were general in their application, the political doctrine was more clearly of relevance to the Court, and the apparent fact that these writers were concerned to reach that particular public is supported by the changing attitude of the Spanish government to the theatre at the time.

During the late sixties the marqués de Grimaldi sought to improve the standards of the public theatre in Madrid by putting on translations of French comedies and tragedies which had already been performed in the court theatres. In 1771 the two companies of players which had previously performed in the Cruz and the Príncipe were reduced to one, to improve the quality of performance, although the reform only lasted a year. This official support for Neo-classical theatre was not long-lived. According to Cotarelo, the conde de Floridablanca reversed the policy in 1777.[26]

The late 1760s and early 1770s therefore gave those Spanish dramatists who were in favour of reform and politically acceptable a unique opportunity. Apart from the elder Moratín and Cadalso, two of the more successful dramatists who used the tragic form are worth discussing here: López de Ayala in his *Numancia destruida*; and Vicente García de la Huerta in his *Agamemnón vengado* and *Raquel*.

Raquel was the first of these plays to be performed, by a scratch amateur company in the North African prison colony at Orán, to which Huerta had been sent on suspicion of writing satires against the conde de Aranda.[27] Although Huerta does not seem to have been proved guilty of subversive activities, there may well have been grounds for suspicion, since *Raquel* itself goes much further than either *Don Sancho García* or *Lucrecia* in inviting nobles to express their opposition to a monarch's conduct; so much so that a censor in 1802 saw it as a dangerously subversive work.[28]

Huerta's approach to the theatre emerges very clearly if his *Raquel* is compared with its most probable source: the seventeenth-century *comedia* by Juan Bautista Diamante, *La judía de Toledo*. Diamante spreads the action over a much longer period, starting indeed from the arrangement of the first meeting between Raquel and the King. He employs a wide range of verse forms, five acts, and a slightly larger cast. Huerta reduces the five acts to three, follows the unities more nearly, and simplifies the verse form radically. All three acts are in assonanted hendecasyllables. Change of assonance is used for dramatic effect in the first two acts; Act I changes from E-A to A-O at the long speech in which García defends himself to the King, and Act II changes from E-A to I-O when Raquel enters to beg clemency from Alfonso; Act III is in E-A assonance throughout. Huerta works into his structure a simple pattern of rises and falls of fortune. Raquel falls from a high point in Act I while García rises; she rises and falls and rises again in Act II, to fall finally in Act III.

In one sense, however, Huerta is nearer the seventeenth-century playwrights than most of his Neo-classic contemporaries. He has a richer poetic vein than either Moratín or Cadalso, and in his *Agamemnón vengado* uses more complex metrical patterns than was common in the 'classical' plays of the period, including his own *Raquel*. In *Raquel* the main sources of emotional intensity are repeated patterns and cumulative sentences; chiasmus is common, and occasionally alliteration is used to rather obvious effect, as in Alfonso's lines in Act II:

> O, títulos pomposos de grandeza,
> sólo sonido, vanidad y viento![29]

In *Agamemnón vengado* we find additional devices such as oxymoron and zeugma, and the metaphorical quality of the verse is more marked.[30] The emotional power of *Raquel*, however, should not be underestimated. Each act has well-organised emotional climaxes within it. Anger, contradiction, and emotional appeals in Act I; the King's laments about court life and threats of suicide in Act II; the tumult of revolt, and the deaths of Rubén and Raquel in Act III; all these sustain the level of intensity and increase it towards the end in a highly effective way. These are not merely theatrical devices, but contribute to the underlying concern with the vagaries of time and justice and the dangers of political ambition.

López de Ayala's *Numancia destruida,* despite its success at the time, seems a lesser work today. No doubt the concessions it makes to spectacle found approval with a wider audience which earlier plays failed to achieve. Ayala seems to be one of the first serious dramatists of the period to give fairly detailed stage directions about the movements of actors and the set. The latter is indeed spectacular, complete with 'un templo extraordinario', a statue of the god Endovélico, an altar with a fire burning, 'sepulcros que rematen en pirámide, después un árbol', and the Roman encampment with trenches. Act II, Scene iv includes a march with the entry of Mancino in chains; Act V is a night scene with burning torches and ultimately the city and temple in flames.

The tragedy itself, as Ayala explains, falls into the category of 'implexas o compuestas', involving great changes of fortune and adversity.[31] Not only does the play follow the changing fortunes of Numancia itself, with its dwindling population, growing hunger, and momentary hope of relief in Act IV, Scene x, it also follows more particularly the changing fortunes of the lovers Olvia and Aluro, who face the choice between sacrificing themselves for the good of their city (literal sacrifice in Aluro's case; sacrifice by giving herself to the Roman general Jugurtha in the case of Olvia), or preserving their love. Their willingness to sacrifice themselves is typical of the people of Numancia as a whole, not merely a patriotic gesture but a will to set liberty before all else. The larger-scale tension, between Numancia and Rome, is also defined in moral terms: the persecuted virtue of Numancia in conflict with the ambition and deceit of Rome. So that ultimately Olvia's and Aluro's choice is emblematic of the city in its entirety.

The treatment of the subject is very different from that of Cervantes's *El cerco de Numancia,* which was published for the first

time shortly after López de Ayala's play.[32] Cervantes is concerned
with changes of fortune and the courage with which individuals and
groups face it. There is a strong patriotic thread in both Cervantes
and López de Ayala, but the latter's main preoccupation seems to be
virtue as the sacrifice of the individual to the collectivity, and concern for the free society. Megara's phrase 'libres nacimos, libres
moriremos' in Act III, Scene vi, is echoed in Act IV, Scene iii by the
communal shout 'Mantengamos/la libertad'. It is not difficult to see
why productions of the play should have embodied liberal aspirations
during Ferdinand VII's absolutist regime.

It is fundamental to Classical tragedy that virtue can suffer. Yet
the frequency with which virtuous individuals other than the protagonist suffer in works of this period in Spain suggests that there
might be a non-literary explanation of the phenomenon. It is tempting
to believe that there may have been some specific political, social, or
even religious situation behind it which is not yet clear from
historians' work of the period. Certainly Ayala himself suggests this
when he dedicates his play to the conde de Aranda who had fallen
from power in 1772 and was ambassador in Paris at the time (1775).
Ayala feels that Aranda will appreciate 'el elogio de aquellos infelices
Españoles, que abandonados por los demás a la ambición Romana,
sólo supieron hallar amparo en la virtud'.[33]

While dramatists in Madrid were stimulated to write tragedies
partly to show foreigners that they could and partly because of
official support from Aranda—Cadalso's *Don Sancho García*, for
instance, was privately performed in Aranda's palace in Madrid and
other tragedies appear to have been put on there too—tragedy was
not entirely neglected in other parts of Spain.[34] In Seville particularly, in the late 1760s and early 70s, while Olavide was *Asistente*,
writers like Trigueros (1736-1800) and Jovellanos appear to have
turned to tragedy. Trigueros's tragedy *El Viting* (or *el Witingo*) was
written before 1770, when its production in Madrid was forbidden
at the same time as that of Cadalso's lost play *Solaya o los Circa-
sianos*.[35] If the text of the undated edition of the play published in
Barcelona by Juan Francisco Piferrer is at all like that seen by the
Madrid censor, the reasons for its banning are fairly clear. The play
partly concerns the attempted regicide of the Emperor of China,
Zunquing, although its pathos stems rather from the unjust persecution, on suspicion of conspiracy, of the innocent Viting, his eldest

son. The conclusion makes a virtue of respect for family and king, and the implication throughout is that heaven supports these traditional values.

In no very real sense is the play subversive or revolutionary, and its artistic appeal must have lain in its exotic *chinoiserie* setting and in certain of its spectacular aspects. The system of versification is simple in the extreme; one assonance pattern for each act, which would probably sound rather monotonous in production.

Jovellanos has a better dramatic sense and a greater emotional range, exploited first in the tragedy *Pelayo* and later in a work which follows the example of the French *comédie larmoyante, El delincuente honrado*.

His *Pelayo* is basically on the same historical subject as Moratín's *Hormesinda*. Like Moratín, Jovellanos is concerned with the story not simply as a tale of tyrannous love but also as a story of the infringement of human rights by occupying powers and absolutism. As Rogundo says to Munuza in Act II, Scene v:

> Y la conquista
> ¿Pudo adquiriros el poder violento
> De profanar los vínculos más santos?
> La fuerza y la invasión hicieron dueño
> De esta ciudad al moro; pero el moro
> Contentó su ambición con el terreno,
> Sin pasar a oprimir nuestro albedrío.
> Y ¿vos queréis, por un culpable exceso,
> Extender el arbitrio de la guerra
> Hasta los corazones?[36]

Jovellanos's argument is a reflection of the Enlightenment's preoccupation with the rights of invaders; a matter about which Spaniards were particularly sensitive, since they were often criticised at this time for the treatment meted out by the conquistadores to South American peoples. He relates the subject closely to personal virtue and a belief in honour and divine justice, and also reflects a non-sectarian view of religion in his sympathetic portrayal of the Moor Achmet.

Jovellanos's *Pelayo* is perhaps little better than *Hormesinda* as drama. The sources of suspense in the plot are more credible, but the language and rhetoric are less flexible: a simple assonance pattern is applied from act to act (I, A-O; II, E-O; III, I-O; IV, A-A; V, A-E), and the usual tricks of repeated patterns, *bimembres*, internal assonance, and cumulative sentences. Like López de Ayala, Jovellanos has a sense of the theatre as spectacle and defines the setting carefully as well as the movements of the characters. He takes the play on emotion further than Nicolás de Moratín. Changes in direction within speeches marked by 'puntos suspensivos', interrupted speeches to assist the build-up of tension—such devices as these are found with far greater frequency in Jovellanos's work.

In fact the *comédie larmoyante* (sentimental drama common in other European countries) is less of a step from *Pelayo* than might at first sight appear. *El delincuente honrado* merely appears very different. Written in prose, not verse, and ending happily, it is set less high in society and has some obviously comic characters. But many of its central preoccupations and some of its sense of theatre are very similar to those we find in Jovellanos's tragedy.

In the first place, the concern with the sense of honour which is at the heart of the problem of the legitimacy of duelling is like that of *Pelayo*. The concern with the emotions is similar. The friendship of Don Anselmo for Don Torcuato; the latter's love for Laura, which she reciprocates; the tender feelings of Don Justo towards Torcuato even before he discovers him to be his natural son, all have counterparts in the tragedy. The devices to build up emotion are basically the same, and much of the language is in the sublime style, close to poetry, full of lines that can be scanned as heptasyllables or hendecasyllables.[37]

There is a major difference, however, between the two works. The tragedy's themes tend to be timeless, whereas those of *El delincuente honrado* are clearly not. At the heart of *El delincuente* is a specific Spanish law passed in 1723 which Jovellanos thought should be amended. Inevitably, as duelling declined in the course of the nineteenth century, the relevance of the play diminished, and it is hard to feel it has much point today. At the same time, some of the central tensions in the play are still perfectly understandable: the conflict between the conservative approach to law of Don Simón, for instance, and the willingness to modify law in the light of a better understanding of human motives, in the case of Don Justo; a conflict repeated in the character of Don Justo himself. This kind of tension is central to Jovellanos's own political attitudes. Though the play is certainly not great drama—characterisation techniques like the careful 'slang' of the servant Felipe creak—as an attempt to convey important topical ideas to a wide public, it is not without interest.

Fundamental to the play is a theory from Montesquieu's *Esprit des lois*: the need to make legal systems appropriate to the climate and customs of the people for whom they are designed. Torcuato states this fairly explicitly in Act I, Scene v. He claims that in Spain there are few lawyers 'que hayan trabajado seriamente en descubrir el espíritu de nuestras leyes', and he goes on to show that honour is the basis of a monarchical society, so the legislation should encourage its existence rather than oppose it. This idea is repeated in Act IV, Scene vi by Justo. Elsewhere we find a critical view of torture (Act II, Scene xiv) which is characteristic of the Enlightenment, as is the attribution of man's behaviour to a combination of his birth and education (Act IV, Scene iii). The sense that the 'hombre de bien' finds tranquillity in the knowledge of his own virtue and the fulfilment of duty, rather than in God or religion, is expressed at the end of Act III, Scene ii, and a belief in reason and humanity in Act III, Scene x. These are a reflection of common Enlightenment ideas. Thus the play, while breaking new aesthetic and ideological ground for Spanish drama, does not put forward any really radical views. Ultimately there is a confidence in the order of the universe, continuing seventeenth-century tradition (Act III, Scene iii); there is respect for the monarchy, and no suggestion that the monarch can do wrong, even though the advice he is given may be suspect.

After Aranda's fall there does not appear to have been the same official encouragement for tragedies, although they continued to be written. Tomás de Iriarte struck out in a new direction in 1791 with his single-character play *Guzmán el Bueno*, which exploited emotional and other tensions within a framework already tried in France by Rousseau, against an evocative musical background in the Handel-Haydn manner, to judge from the published fragments.[38]

Cienfuegos also plays on the emotions, in a more obvious way than Cadalso's generation. In his variations on the theme of the latter's *Don Sancho García*, for instance, entitled *La Condesa de Castilla*, the Condesa has been tricked into falling in love with the Moor Almanzor, who had killed her husband. Her son Sancho, discovering her relationship with the Moor, condemns her to a convent (Act III, Scene iii). She then attempts to poison Sancho out of anger, not for love of the

Moor as in Cadalso's play, and finally takes the cup and drinks of her own free will, not under compulsion. Fate plays a greater part in her situation than in that of Cadalso's Condesa, whose passions are wholly responsible for her difficulties. There is in Cienfuegos's heroine more injured innocence than guilty passion.

As one would expect from his poetry, Quintana in his tragedies gives even fuller rein to the imagination and the senses. *El Duque de Viseo* is set in a fortress and its dungeon, and the second act takes place at night. There is a dream sequence in Act II, Scene v to which prominence is given by a special assonance pattern, which elsewhere changes only once in each act, and here changes twice within the scene (E-A; O-A; I-O). Politically too *El Duque de Viseo* is an advance on previous tragedies. Duke Enrique, who has usurped the throne from his brother Eduardo, is punished for his amorous and political tyranny at the end by death—suicide. There are precedents for this, of course, but not for the exploitation of his conscience in Act III, Scene v and in the dream scene. This sequence is no doubt a restrained version of the ghost scene in Matthew Lewis's *The Castle Spectre*, from which the play clearly derives its plot if not its detail.[39] Quintana's approach to the adaptation of Lewis's play shows a concern for restraint that is far from the Gothic original. Also in Quintana's play there are some pointed comments on the enslavement of coloured people by whites, occurring in scenes involving Ali and Asán. They have abundant justification for hatred and express their feeling early in the play, without the author feeling it necessary to condemn their attitude.

Quintana's *Pelayo* (1805), following Jovellanos's play of the same title and Moratín's *Hormesinda* in its choice of subject, protests against religious tyranny. He also shows a deeper interest than his predecessors in motivation, and makes Hormesinda a complex character who accepts Munuza's hand to save her countrymen from persecution, and then sticks to her marriage out of a sense of duty. The stress and conflict of her situation is therefore much greater than in the earlier plays, in which she was suspected but not guilty of collaboration. The stress is given visible expression in her faint in Act II, Scene i after her marriage; her tense scene with her brother (Act II, Scene vi); her vision of Pelayo in Act IV, Scene i; and her final confrontation with Pelayo and death at the end of Act V; it is also pointed by the rhetoric of the play.

The question of collaboration with the enemy or the tyrant—a marginal one in most of these plays—obviously acquired new significance at the time of the Peninsular War. Martínez de la Rosa makes it an important topic in his *Viuda de Padilla*, written in Cadiz in about 1812. The parallel between the *comuneros* in sixteenth-century Segovia, struggling to maintain their rights against Charles V whose yoke was made by 'codiciosos extranjeros' (Act I, Scene i), and the struggle of the Spanish against foreign-backed oppression in the Peninsular War is obvious. The main tension in the play is between the Viuda de Padilla, to whom freedom is precious above all things, and her father-in-law Pedro López de Padilla and Don Pedro Laso de la Vega, both of whom argue that prudence and commonsense force the *comuneros* to capitulate. At the end of Act III the widow still carries the people with her, but in Act IV Laso plots against her, and at the end of the final act she commits suicide rather than submit to the enemy. The plot is simple and, despite the implications of the subject, played out in an upper-class setting. Since the play is focused on the widow, there is less sense of the problems of a community than in López de Ayala's *Numancia destruida*, which, as we have already remarked, enjoyed some success at the Peninsular War period. Martínez de la Rosa posed his problems in terms of individual morality rather than in group terms. Nevertheless, the legitimacy of rebellion against the king is much more explicit here than in any of the earlier tragedies we have discussed, since the issue is not confused, as earlier dramatists (including Quintana) tended to make it, by presenting it as a Spanish-Moorish conflict.

From the point of view of techniques, however, Martínez de la Rosa is less adventurous than Quintana. He uses the by now inevitable assonanted hendecasyllables, changing assonance only with each new act (I, E-O; II, A-O; III, A-A; IV, E-A; V, E-O). Whether the return in the last act to the assonance of the first was intended to be functional it is difficult to say. Theoretically it might be felt that it helped to give the tragedy a closed-circle effect, though in practice it would hardly be noticed. There is, however, one interesting technique in the play which is worth mentioning—the use of darkness. Night pieces are not uncommon in earlier tragedies; in Quintana they seem to provide a counterpart for the dark forces in the play. In Martínez de la Rosa their symbolic function is still clearer. The widow's triumph (Act III) and the previous acts take place by day; the last two, in which the collaborators plot and have their way, take place by night.

By the early years of the nineteenth century the tragedy was an established form. Evidence suggests that Quintana's were not unsuccessful. Certainly he was not deterred by their reception or inclined to give up the genre, and he relates that three further tragedies were in an advanced state of completion in 1808—*Roger de Flor*, *El Príncipe de Viana*, and *Blanca de Borbón*.[40] Possibly the assimilation of techniques from the ever-popular spectacular theatre helped works like those by López de Ayala and Quintana to reach a public which did not normally accept tragedy. Possibly too the frequent performance of tragedies had, at least by the time that Quintana was writing, created a new and wider public for serious drama.

The more obviously popular theatre, however, remained, as always, comic. At the time when the elder Moratín and his contemporaries were writing tragedies, there developed a new skill at writing short amusing plays to precede or run between the acts of longer ones. A writer in this genre was Ramón de la Cruz (1731-94), who proved a failure as a writer of full-length drama. He was familiar, however, with all dramatic forms, and with Italian as well as French and Spanish works. His familiarity with Spanish contemporary tragedy is particularly reflected in parody form in *Manolo* (1769), which he describes as 'tragedia para reír o sainete para llorar'. Written in the inevitable assonanted hendecasyllables, *Manolo* includes all the rhetorical techniques of parallel structures, 'gradación' (cumulative sentences), invocation of the gods ('¡Oh santos Dioses! Yo te juro, ¡ah perra!'),[41] and *bimembres* ('la llave saques y el candil enciendas'),[42] to make the audience laugh. The characters all fall dead one after another in the last scene.

Yet it should not be supposed that tragedy is being mocked by Cruz, any more than it should be assumed that Pope is mocking the epic in *The Rape of the Lock*, or Sánchez Barbero mocking Garcilaso in his burlesque on the Inquisition already mentioned.[43] The object seems to be to mock the behaviour of *majos* by making them ape the manners of the upper class. Incongruity of style gives rise to irony. The characters are not dressed in the manner of tragic actors but in low-life costume, making the effect of what they say more ridiculous. It is in fact the kind of comedy in which the behaviour of people who are obviously different from the mainly sophisticated members of the audience is ridiculed; and the audience laughs at characters rather than sees the relevance of them. *Muñuelo* is a diluted sequel to *Manolo* as a parody of tragedy, and there is a comparable parody of Golden Age heroic drama in *Los bandos del Avapiés y la venganza del zurdillo*, where war between *majos* of the Lavapiés and Barquillo districts of Madrid is reminiscent of opposing factions of earlier plays.[44] The take-off of the style of Calderonian drama in this instance is sharpened by apposite rhetorical tricks. The type of high-flown address to assembled nobles—the Queen addressing the Caravajales and Benavides in Act I, Scene ix of Tirso's *La prudencia en la mujer*, for instance—is humorously imitated by Pelundris and Canillejas in the opening street-scene of *Los bandos del Avapiés* in parallel speeches, the second of which begins:

> *Canillejas* : Grandes, invencibles héroes,
> que en los ejércitos diestros
> de borrachera, rapiña,
> gatería y vítuperio,
> fatigáis las faltriqueras,
> las tabernas y los juegos,
> venid a escuchar el modo
> de vengar nuestro desprecio.

In the same play there is a further parody of Golden Age techniques in a passage in which different voices take up fragments of nearly each line of verse in rapid exchanges:

> *Zaina* : No le mates.
> *Zurdillo* :   Ya me tengo.
> *Canillejas* : Que es tu enemigo.
> *Zurdillo* :   ¡Bien dices!
> *Zaina* : Que es mi sangre.
> *Zurdillo* :   Ya lo veo.
> *Canillejas* : Derrámala.
> *Zurdillo* :   Será justo.
> *Zaina* : No hagas tal.
> *Zurdillo* :   Será bien hecho.
> *Canillejas* : Yo tu amigo te lo pido.
> *Zaina* : Yo tu esposa te lo ruego.

Possibly the parody of the seventeenth-century theatre, and in this instance of eighteenth-century tragedy too, is also reflected in the questions of honour among *majos* and *majas* which often arise in Cruz's *sainetes*.

One very good explanation for these parodies lies in the fact that the *sainete* was performed for light relief between the acts of the main play of the evening. The telescoped play within a play in *La visita de duelo* (1768) gives a fairly clear idea of the normal course of events at an eighteenth-century theatrical performance. In a three-act play, a *loa* precedes the first act, an *entremés* and *tonadilla* the second, and a *sainete* and *tonadilla* the third. In Cruz's time theatrical wit rather than the illusion of reality had become the norm for the shorter pieces, even using actors as themselves on occasion.[45] There seems to have been a greater variety of entertainment than had usually been the case in the seventeenth century. Calderón's concept of the *loa*, for example, as something that could be thematically linked to the main play or in a sense explanatory of it (like Molière's *Intermèdes* for *Georges Dandin*) seems to have been forgotten. More common is the amusing piece which either has no relation to the main play or does not attempt to sustain its illusion. Vicente García de la Huerta's *loa* for a performance of *La vida es sueño*, put on in Orán by officers and officials of the garrison, pretends that the person who was to play Rosaura did not want to perform.[46] There is an obvious in-joke here (Rosaura was certainly played by a man, presumably by one of the officers) which is emphasised when the character asks the audience if she/he can leave through the pit.

Writers of tragedy naturally did not appreciate these jokes, and it may have been felt that Cruz was mocking the political establishment in making fun of tragedy, the dramatic form with which the government was chiefly identified. Certainly an anonymous attack on foreign politicians and generals in power in Spain after the abortive Algiers expedition in 1775 was written as a parody of tragedy.[47]

Apart from his works of parody Cruz largely follows seventeenth-century precedents in his *sainetes*. He uses the bad Spanish of the *vizcaíno* as a conventional source of humour in *La maja majada*, and follows the tradition of Cervantes, Quiñones de Benavente, and others in taking his subjects mostly from low-life, the *demi-monde* of prostitutes or near-prostitutes, the gallants who pursue them, and rustics. Yet there are a number of new developments in Cruz's *sainetes*. For one thing, the visual side of his theatre is more generously treated, in accordance with the eighteenth-century interest in spectacle. There is often one quite major scene change of an ambitious nature within these relatively short works. *La pradera de San Isidro*, for instance, opens in a 'salón corto', and then moves to the 'pradera' itself with the chapel of San Isidro in the background, and a line of parked coaches, flats with 'selva', and one or two trees around which people are grouped. A live donkey and a crying baby are also specified, and 'seguidillas que canta el coro y bailan los majos ordinarios, y al mismo tiempo llora el niño y rebuzna el burro'. *La Plaza Mayor* starts with 'calle o selva' and then opens to reveal the Plaza Mayor of Madrid complete with street-cries, etc. Many of the plays move from a street-scene to an interior, or from one interior to another. Cruz adds to the varying rhythm and movement of his productions by alternating small groups and large groups, dialogue and song, or song and dance, so that the movements of characters as well as the sets enrich the visual spectacle. In *La Petra y la Juana o el buen casero*, also called *La casa de Tócame Roque*, the set is a patio with fountain, balconies at first-floor level, and two attic windows out of which the characters lean and speak. A cat with a chicken in its mouth is required to walk across the roofs near the attics at one point in the action. . . .

It is easy to see why the plays were immensely popular in Cruz's time, as they were too in the nineteenth century with those who admired *costumbrismo* or who thought his works realistic.[48] Cruz's concern, however, is not with the recording and illustration of *costumbres* so much as with their picturesque quality. He chooses the exceptional moment rather than the ordinary, and likes to show characters reacting to particular moments of hate, greed, or love rather than to the humdrum mixture of the everyday. Indeed he readily distorts the everyday in order to make his points clear; and his exaggerated portrayal of amorous *abates*, *majos*, and *majas*, and of the middle-class gentlemen trying to win the favours of the latter, is strongly moralistic. *Abates*, foolish gentlemen, and uncontrolled low-life characters are all mocked by Cruz. Although gentlefolk in Cervantine tradition are often enough the object of Cruz's satire—a fact which might well account for some of the opposition to his plays—generally speaking he liked to keep the hierarchical arrangement of Spanish society as it always had been. There is less criticism of absentee landlords in *Las frioleras*, for instance, than of the *nouveaux riches* of country villages and the immoral self-seekers who have no standards and no consideration for others. In *La presumida burlada* the presumptuous one-time serving-maid is taught her place by her upper-class husband. And a similarly traditionalist pattern is reflected in *El petimetre*, in the satirical view taken of Zoilo's enthusiasm for new and foreign fashions, which, in the author's view, debilitate the country.

Far more challenging intellectually and socially are the serious comedies of Leandro Fernández de Moratín (1760-1828). No earlier comic writer in the century achieved the same success with theatre audiences. But writers of the previous generation had attempted to establish Neo-classic comedy as well as tragedy, and Nicolás Fernández de Moratín's *Petimetra* (1762), already discussed, was followed by three comedies by Tomás de Iriarte: *El don de gentes o la habanera, La señorita malcriada,* and *El señorito mimado.*

Iriarte's plays are all interesting thematically, but hardly broke new ground from the dramatic point of view. In *El don de gentes* the value of virtue and education as opposed to social status appears to be asserted, also the need for reason and control rather than exaggeration. The characters tend towards extremes, as Doña Elena describes them in Act I, Scene i: Don Alberto is too old-fashioned, Leandro too formal, Melchior too indifferent, the Barón de Sotobello too frivolous; he tries everything modern. Leandro falls in love with the maid Rosalía and does not worry about her status:

> Ya me canso
> De repetir que tan sólo
> Reconozco aquellos grados
> De distinción que en las almas
> Fija la virtud.

But the apparent egalitarianism loses some of its force when Rosalía turns out to be the cousin of the Barón. The dramatic element here is chiefly maintained by means of *enredo*, twists and turns of the plot. And it was in this respect that Leandro Fernández de Moratín's work was to mark a considerable development.

Iriarte's *El señorito mimado*, as its subtitle tells us, is about 'la mala educación'. Don Mariano, who has been spoilt by his mother, leads an idle pointless existence. Mentally, as his uncle Don Cristóbal (the voice of reason) points out, he is living in the past, even believ-

ing in ghosts and alchemy. The inevitable love interest is fairly inci-
dental and the contrasts between rational and irrational characters are
very simple, although the commitment of the man of reason to social
activity is effectively brought out. The man of substance is no use
unless he contributes to the society in which he lives. *La señorita
malcriada*, Iriarte's other *comedia moral*, is again rather simply
organised. There is a stock rustic character (Tío Pedro), some danc-
ing with *majos* and *majas*, and exploitation of linguistic humour in
the globe-trotting Marqués de Fontecalda who writes Frenchified
Spanish and belongs to the Arcades de Roma under the name of
Olocosmo Girabundo. Reason in the shape of Don Eugenio, a factory-
manager, struggles against the Marqués, whose conduct is as unreasonable as his language. In this work the defence of the active, commercial middle class is taken somewhat further than it had been in
El don de gentes. The idle rich, like Don Gonzalo, and the Marqués
de Fontecalda, the aristocratic floater, are shown not only to be useless
in society but also dangerous: the Marqués is crooked, and Don
Gonzalo is easily deceived by him. The latter's irrational approach to
life passes on to his ill-educated spoilt daughter, who also takes things
at their face value and gives way to all her momentary passions.
'Good' characters like Don Eugenio are victims of both, and true
status is achieved by virtue and reason, not by birth, as in *El don de
gentes*.

> La conducta
> Es la que humilla o exalta.   (Dona Clara, Act I, Scene iv)

The younger Moratín takes the preoccupation with social values
and Enlightenment ideas much further, and also develops a subtler
dramatic form. The subjects are similar to those of Iriarte: education, truth, reason, social justice, and the passions; but the characters
are much more complex.

El viejo y la niña, the earliest of the five original plays, is also the
least subtle in form and content.[49] At first sight it seems to be an
eighteenth-century reworking of a typical Golden Age plot, exploiting
a triangular situation with elderly husband (Roque), young wife
(Isabel), and young man (Juan) who had been in love with the wife
in the past and has returned to find her married. The suspense
mechanism is primitive. The first act starts with the suspicions of
Roque, which are confirmed as far as Juan's feelings towards Isabel

are concerned in Scene iv, while Isabel confesses that she reciprocates his love in Scene xi. The first act leaves the audience with Juan's determination to leave Spain, and Isabel's appeal that he should stay. Act II continues the suspense, holding back the second confrontation between Isabel and Juan until Scene xi, when Isabel once again begs Juan to stay, yet resists the temptation to accept his love; she calls him back, however, in Scene xiv. Act III holds up his return until Scene x, when there is a third confrontation in which Isabel is forced to tell Juan to go after all because Roque is watching the interview. A final meeting two scenes later, when Juan is about to embark, shows Isabel confessing her love yet again, but tragically determined to enter a convent.

The suspense-mechanism is helped out by a kind of sub-plot: Roque's treatment of his sister Beatriz and her relationship with Isabel. Comic scenes between Roque and his servant Muñoz spin out the action. There is an artificial parallel between Acts II and III, in the first of which Muñoz watches Juan and Isabel from a place of concealment, and in the second of which Roque does the same thing.

Thematically, though, the play is very different from seventeenth-century prototypes. Morality is important, but honour is not. Roque is less concerned for his honour than for the possible loss of a wife who is part of his worldly goods and a useful contributor to the comforts of his old age. His preoccupations are material not social. The *honrada* quality of his previous wives lay in their good house-keeping qualities (Act I, Scene viii). The Cadiz mercantile back-ground is very relevant to the basic conflict between the financial obsessions of Roque and the human emotions of Isabel and Juan. Roque's character is seen almost wholly in terms of commercial greed; a perversion of feeling. His meanness and tyranny towards Beatriz and his enslavement of Isabel are reflections of this. Juan's uncle's business affairs originally caused the separation of Juan and Isabel: Isabel's tutor's preference for the financially advantageous marriage with Roque is ultimately responsible for the tragic situation. Thus Juan and Isabel, and Beatriz too in a way, are the victims of inhuman values (oppression, slavery, material greed) which respect neither true sentiments nor virtue.

This setting of human qualities and conflicts in the context of social morality and conventions is characteristic of Moratín's work. So is the concern with deep feeling, hardly a *forte* in Iriarte's comedies. Already in *El viejo y la niña* Moratín makes extensive use of changes of direction, uncompleted sentences, and pauses within speeches; characters often interrupt one another, so creating a sense of emotional tension through dialogue. The basic situation itself is of course highly emotional, and both Isabel and Beatriz have to struggle to keep their emotions under control. The play might be said to be about the perversion and martyrdom of natural feelings, and this seems to be Moratín's central preoccupation.

In this instance a guardian was responsible for the martyrdom of Isabel. In the other major comedies, with the exception of *La comedia nueva*, parents are responsible. A particularly interesting case is that of *La mojigata*, where the obstinacy, egoism, and rigour of Martín's upbringing of his daughter Clara turn her into a deceiver and a religious hypocrite. Greed for money is again a force in this play. Claudio, a wastrel, is as willing to deceive as Clara in order to obtain it. Yet neither Claudio nor Clara are wholly to blame for the way they are. Claudio's father lives by tricky too, and has exercised no control over his son, as Claudio reveals in Act II, Scene xiv; Don Martín also is morally as well as educationally reprehensible, since he encourages his daughter in her supposed religious leanings so that he can have the money she expects to inherit, according to Perico in Act I, Scene iii. The underlying conception here is very like that of Mor de Fuentes's *La Serafina*: virtue must be social. As Doña Inés says in the last scene:

> si la virtud consiste
> en acciones, no en palabras,
> hagamos bien....
>   No quiero riquezas
> si no he de saber usarlas
> en amparar infelices . . .
> ¡Oh maldito el que las haga
> estériles y perece
> sobre el tesoro que guarda!

Additionally, social virtues are not absolutes but can be achieved by appealing to self-interest when virtuous impulse fails (cf. Pope's *Essay on Man*). As Don Luis puts it, when speaking of Clara:

Si en ella estímulos faltan
de honor, hará el interés
lo que la virtud no alcanza.

That human nature is a mixed force, with potentialities for good as
well as evil, is a fundamental theme in Moratín's work. Morality is
designed to ensure that human nature is allowed reasonable outlets
without harming others. Restraint but not repression is the ideal. In
El sí de las niñas this is very clearly developed. When too much
restraint is applied, basically good young people like Doña Paquita
and Carlos start misbehaving, as Paquita does in the convent. Furthermore, the restricted upbringing and the pressures exerted on Paquita
by her mother make it difficult for her to admit the truth. Their
egoism, channelled into marriage, will become good; their self-love
hard to distinguish from love for each other. With Don Diego and
Doña Irene, however, we have instances of egoism which goes near to
ruining the lives of others. It is clear from the first scene that Diego
wants someone to look after him rather than a wife to love. Doña
Irene has not learnt from her own unhappy experience of marriage,
and is more concerned that Paquita should do her bidding than that
she should be happy.

The balance of love and self-love is a difficult one to strike, just as
it is sometimes difficult to make the interests of the individual com-
patible with those of society. The language of Moratín's plays
suggests that perhaps his family relationships are to be understood as
microcosms, illustrating the larger problems of tyranny, oppression,
slavery, freedom, and equality. Certainly this would be in keeping
with the practice of the period, in which family relationships are
often taken as a model for those within the state; love is seen, in
Cienfuegos and Mor de Fuentes for example, as an essential force for
the cohesion of society.[50]

But it is not only in the field of ideas that Moratín's plays are of
interest. Within the framework of Neo-classicism he polished and
refined the form of the Spanish comedy, and did so in ways which
were to leave an imprint for over half a century. In his verse-plays he
continues the convention of his period, using *romance* as his basic
form and changing assonance only from act to act. He adheres rigidly
to the unities of time and place and reduces the *enredo* element to a
minimum. Such complications as there are tend to be introduced with

almost mathematical exactitude in the last few scenes of each act. Yet
Moratín makes obvious concessions to popular taste for spectacle and
traditional suspense devices: the character lying hidden and watching
the action in *El viejo y la niña*; the blundering-about of characters on
a darkened stage during the siesta in *La mojigata*, and in Act III of
El sí de las niñas in a night scene. Another visually pleasing passage
is the dawning of day in the same act.

These concessions to popular taste, however, are in reality very
relevant to the struggle between forces of reason and unreason in
Moratín's plays. A similarly symbolic effect is achieved in Part I of
La comedia nueva by the chaotic noise coming from an upstairs
room in the café, where Eleuterio, his wife, and friends ('locos
poetas') are celebrating the approach of the first performance of *El
gran cerco de Viena* with a lunch. *La comedia nueva* also illustrates
the effective way in which Moratín can use sound and language to
create both tension and spectacle. And in this play, in which Spain's
status in the world and happiness within the family are both seen to
depend on rationality, there is no gross oversimplification of the
struggle between reason and unreason. By giving characters a variety
of language and expression, Moratín shows a broader spectrum of
attitudes than in any of his other plays with the exception of *El sí de
las niñas*. Tending to one extreme we have Don Hermógenes (unreason) and to the other Don Pedro (reason).[51] Middle characters are
Don Serapio, Don Eleuterio, and his wife on the unreasonable side;
and Doña Mariquita (lower bourgeoisie) and Don Antonio (upper
bourgeoisie) on the side of reason. The avoidance of any one absolute
personification of the 'voice of reason' continues in *El sí de las niñas*
where Don Diego is seen to be acting irrationally in the first scene of
the play—his servant Simón is more rational than he at that point—
but later becoming more reasonable.

The creation of interest through variety in speech is extended into
the detail of all the plays. Dramatic tension is instantly created at the
beginning of *La mojigata*, for instance, in an angry exchange between
Don Martín and Don Luis. Similar dramatic exchanges in *El sí de
las niñas* occur between Don Diego and Don Carlos in Act III,
Scene x, shortly after a more emotional exchange between Don Diego
and Paquita (Scene viii) and just before a highly comic and emotional
argument between Don Diego and Doña Irene (Scene xi). All the
plays are full of changes of direction, pauses within speeches, and

interruptions, which contribute to the emotional content as well as to the rhythm of the action.

The importance of human feeling which is fundamental to Moratín's conception of life is aptly reflected in these emotional passages and devices. The exploitation of the emotions in tragedy at the same period made new demands on actors and actresses. Acting standards had been the subject of considerable concern on the part of the government and intellectuals in the late 1760s. A French director, Louis Reynaud, was appointed at that period with a brief which included orders to clean up *sainetes*, ensure that actors did not *ad lib* and add words to their parts, were adequately rehearsed and disciplined, and performed more naturally than had been their wont.[52] Inappropriate dress and an exaggerated manner seem to have been common, and to judge from Leandro Fernández de Moratín's anecdotal description of his father's problems with the actors when *Hormesinda* was in rehearsal, there was no great willingness to try new dramatic styles. Within the next forty years there must have been some developments, yet further reforms advocated by the younger Moratín and Santos Díez González needed to be officially backed in 1798. A book published in Madrid in 1800 speaks of the need to give acting the status of a liberal art, since actors must not just learn their parts in a mechanised way, but must also be able to interpret character. A good production required 'una buena declamación de los papeles, con todos los matices, y con toda la acción y juego mudo que exigen las situaciones y la expresión propia de cada pasión'.[53] The author of this book goes on to explain in detail the nature of the passions and the gestures appropriate to them, with the aid of a series of etchings to illustrate twenty different facial expressions and poses. In the early years of the nineteenth century much of this theory was translated into practice on the Madrid stage by Isidoro Máiquez (1768-1820) and his company. Máiquez had studied the great Talma's craft in Paris in 1799 and successfully adapted the techniques of the French style to Spanish tastes on his return.

Despite the improvements in acting and presentation, dramatists in Spain continued to face the eternal problem of the theatre: the conflict between public taste and the minority appeal of new work. Sometimes this general issue takes specifically Spanish forms: the struggle between European-style theatre and national Golden Age traditions, for instance; the conflicting loyalties of the supporters of the companies playing at the Cruz and the Príncipe in Madrid—the famous *Chorizos* and *Polacos*. It is clear that the dramatists we have so far discussed made some concessions to popular taste. Others were prepared to go much further. Moratín, in *La comedia nueva*, mocks a play which is supposedly preoccupied with Classical techniques (verisimilitude, etc.) and yet is in reality attempting to excite the audience through spectacle. Certainly Comella (1751-1812), whom Moratín seems to have been attacking, had no qualms about making frequent scene changes, devising twisting and turning plots, spectacular battles, or marches and countermarches on the stage, and accompanying it all with music. Comella's *El sitio de Calés* (1790), supposedly the object of Moratín's satire in *La comedia nueva*, was probably based on the French dramatist Belloy's patriotic and emotional play of the same title, which lent itself to an increase in the spectacular element. In 1784 Forner complained in a letter to López de Ayala that the censors should allow plays to be put on like 'una comedia disparatada de Moncín en que un ejército de Roncalesas salían a caballo en yeguas en son de mojiganga para urdir a los mozos una estratagema obscenamente estrafalaria'.[54] These popular dramatists were not continuing the Golden Age traditions so much as popularising the new practices of their own times. Comella, for instance, had particular success with the *comédie larmoyante* genre in his *Cecilia* (1786) and *Cecilia viuda* (1787); so did Gaspar de Zabala y Zamora in *Las víctimas del amor: Ana y Sindham* (1789).[55]

Particularly interesting is the way in which these plays by more popular dramatists pick up and transmit some of the ideas of the Enlightenment. The enlightened despot is part of the subject-matter of Comella's *Federico II, Rey de Prusia, Federico II en el campo de Torgau, Federico en Glatz*, and *El Fénix de los ingenios o María Teresa de Austria*. In the second of the three Frederick II plays the central topic is a criticism of torture, much debated at the time in Spain in published work, and, in the case of Forner, in unpublished work too. The younger Moratín's favourite subject—arranged marriages—is also central to Comella's *El matrimonio por razón de estado* (1794), in which a husband and wife are both victims of their parents' whims and in consequence live miserably together and seek solace elsewhere. Yet there is a clear difference of approach between Moratín and Comella: the former is more interested in investigating causes, the latter in making dramatic capital out of effects. Some plays

by these lesser-known eighteenth-century dramatists also attempted
to deal with the broader questions of the hierarchical society, a central
preoccupation of the Enlightenment, particularly after Rousseau's
Discours sur l'inégalité. We have already seen how the rights of
individuals in society were upheld against tyrants or abusers of the
social system in a number of Neo-classical tragedies. Passages in
Huerta's *Raquel* refer to the meaninglessness of noble titles, as do
passages in Tomás de Iriarte's comedies. Leandro Fernández de
Moratín's *El Barón* shows the stupidity of assuming that a title is any
indication of real worth; and Cadalso's Tediato in the *Noches
lúgubres* speaks of 'arbitrarias e inútiles clases'.

A minor dramatist called Bázquez wrote an interesting one-act
comedia called *El salvaje americano*[56] which appears not to have been
put on, and which may have disturbed the censor by its frank egalitarianism. The main character of the play is Levin, an Indian—the
Noble Savage beloved of the Enlightenment—who looks at Spanish
society with an innocent eye. The injustice of wealth and the ability
of reason to guide man to a right knowledge of good and evil are
important themes in the play, and clear reflections of Enlightenment
principles. So of course is the conception of the Noble Savage
embodied in Levin; a not uncommon figure in European drama at
the time, though rare in Spain.

One other way in which the popular dramatists reflect their more
serious contemporaries is in the development of an obviously middle-
class theatre. Leandro Fernández de Moratín's plays are perhaps
primarily concerned with the untitled nobility: the *hidalgo* class
which held posts in the government offices, commercial enterprises,
and the army at the period. The lower middle-class world of clerks
emerges occasionally—as in Don Eleuterio in *La comedia nueva*—
but is seen from above as a group to be encouraged and patronised,
but not liberated. Yet Moratín explicitly advised writers to seek 'en
la clase media de la sociedad los argumentos, los personajes, los
caracteres, las pasiones y el estilo en que debe expresarlas'.[57] His
views were no doubt shared by Cándido María Trigueros, whose
prizewinning play *Los menestrales* was put on in Madrid in 1784 to
celebrate the birth of two Infantes and the conclusion of peace nego-
tiations with Great Britain. Trigueros takes the common view of the
period that true nobility lies in usefulness to society rather than in
titles. But high society still precedes low and 'tan bueno es el

alto como el bajo';[58] the artisan should not aspire to rise above his station.

Latent in many of the plays of this period, both comedy and tragedy, is a movement towards a different and less hierarchical society, a sense of the injustice of the *status quo*. Latent also is the discussion of morality in social rather than religious terms. Ecclesiastical and government censorship no doubt held many ideas in check. Yet there is the sense that authors were beginning to express unconventional as well as conventional viewpoints, to speak for minorities —and not merely ruling minorities—as well as for the majority. But the theatre more than any other literary genre in the eighteenth century tends to set aside one kind of tyranny only to accept another: exchanging the patronage of kings and nobles for that of popular taste.

NOTES

1. See A. D. Coe, *Catálogo bibliográfico y crítico de las comedias anunciadas en los periódicos de Madrid desde 1661 hasta 1819* (Baltimore, 1935). For a partial study of the theatre in Seville, see F. Aguilar Piñal, *Cartelera prerromántica Sevillana, Años 1800–1836* (Madrid, 1968).
2. José Subirá, *El teatro del Real Palacio (1849–1851)* (Madrid, 1950), pp. 17–103.
3. E. Cotarelo y Mori, *María del Rosario Fernández. La Tirana* (Madrid, 1897), pp. 6 *et seq.*
4. See René Andioc, *Sur la querelle du théâtre au temps de Leandro Fernández de Moratín* (Bordeaux, 1970).
5. *Discurso sobre las tragedias españolas* (Madrid, 1750), p. 71.
6. *Diario Pinciano*, No. 2, sábado, 2 de febrero de 1788, p. 13.
7. *Angélica y Medoro de Cañizares*, ed. Julius A. Molinaro and Warren T. McCready (Turin, 1958), pp. 11-12. Fifteen verse changes in Act I and sixteen in Act III are noted.
8. S. G. Morley, 'The curious phenomenon of Spanish verse drama', in *BH*, L (1948), 443–62.
9. José Cadalso, *Suplemento al papel intitulado Los eruditos a la violeta*, Boileau section—'me acuerdo haber visto una comedia famosa (así lo decía el cartel) en que el Cardenal Cisneros con todas sus reverencias iba de Madrid a Orán, y volvía de Orán a Madrid en un abrir y cerrar de ojos; allí había ángeles y diablos, cristianos y moros, mar y corte, Africa y Europa, &c. &c.; y bajaba Santiago en un caballo blanco y daba cuchilladas al aire matando tanto perro moro, que era un consuelo para mí y para todo buen soldado cristiano; por señas que se descolgó un angelón de madera de los de la comitiva del campeón celeste, y por poco mata medio patio lleno de cristianos viejos que estábamos con las bocas abiertas.'
10. *Comedia nueva. Pluma, púrpura y espada sólo en Cisneros se halla* (Madrid, 1740), *passim.*

11. Luzán, *La poética* (Madrid, 1789), I, 92. In Barcelona, 1956, ed. p. 22 in vol. I.

12. A typical view is that expressed in the anonymous *Théâtre espagnol* (Paris, 1770), I, xxv: 'C'est que les espagnols n'en font point [des tragédies] ou du moins qu'il n'est pas possible de les distinguer des drames, dont le sujet est plus commun.'

13. See David Williams, *Voltaire as literary critic*, in *Studies on Voltaire and the Eighteenth Century*, ed. T. Besterman, Vol. XLVIII (Geneva, 1966), 252 *et seq.*

14. Luzán, *La poética*, I, 100. In Barcelona, 1956, ed. I, 92.

15. See Otis H. Green, 'La dignidad real en la literatura del siglo de oro: notículas de un estudioso', *RFE*, XLVIII (1965), 231–50.

16. See J. Marías, *La España posible en tiempo de Carlos III* (Madrid, 1963), pp. 174-5.

17. See Leandro Fernández de Moratín's view of the 'ambiguity' of his father's comedy from a stylistic point of view in his Prólogo (*Obras de D. Leandro Fernández de Moratín* (Madrid, 1830), II, Comedias originales, Parte Primera, xxxiii-xxxiv.

18. *BAE*, 2, p. 97 b.

19. ibid., p. 91 a/b.

20. ibid., p. 105 a.

21. See Leandro Fernández de Moratín's *Vida* of his father, *BAE*, 2, p. x.

22. *BAE*, 2, p. 131a.

23. Luzán's *Poética*, Book II, chapter 3: 'El poeta puede, y debe siempre que tenga ocasión oportuna instruir a sus lectores, ya en la moral con máximas y sentencias graves que siembra en sus versos, ya en la política con los discursos de un ministro en una Tragedia.' As instances of Montiano's practice we take the following:

> *Ataulpho*: que la Fortuna más que no de cuerdos
> suele dejarse halar de temerarios;
> y en el concepto de la plebe nunca
> le faltó la razón a la victoria.
>
> o cuántas
> luces ofusca la pasión.
>
> A los grandes Imperios, Sigerico,
> la Espada, que los funda, los destruye,
> si la razón sus filos no gobierna.
> (Act I, Scene v)
> ¡Qué veloz se nos huye la fortuna!
> ¡Qué breves son los gustos, con que premia!
> (Act II, Scene vi)
>
> *Virginia*: La ceguedad por lo común no acierta:
> la pausa las más veces lo consigue.
> (Act I, Scene iv)
> Quien aspira a lograr lo que apetece,
> huye de los escrúpulos cobardes.
> Máximas de reparo u de recelo,
> No las sigue jamás el poderoso.
> (Act III, Scene i)

24. Apart from following the unities, Cadalso appears to take from Aristotelian theory the devices of Discovery and Suffering, and the cause of his

tragedy lies 'not in any depravity, but in some great error' as the *Art of Poetry* required. He has obviously noted Aristotle's affirmation that 'when murder or the like is done or meditated . . . by mother on son, or son on mother—these are the situations the poet should seek after'.

25. op. cit., II, 22.

26. E. Cotarelo y Mori, *María del Rosario Fernández. La Tirana*, p. 11.

27. See J. Asensio's article in *Estudios*, XVIII (1962), 507-11; and F. Aguilar Piñal, 'Las primeras representaciones de la "Raquel" de García de la Huerta', *RL*, 63 and 64, 1967 (1969), 133-6.

28. See P. Demerson, 'Un escándalo en Cuenca', in *BRAH*, XLIX, 317–28. Some of the variants noted by J. G. Fucilla in his edition of the play (Santander—Madrid—Barcelona, 1965) suggest that the original version may have been still more subversive. See for example note 13 (ibid., p. 28): 'Los Reyes, Reyes son, para ser justos: / que no hay razón que al soberano exima / del delito que lo es en el vasallo: / y sí al contrario, el vicio que sería / acaso disculpable en las Cabañas / si en los Palacios reina, escandaliza . . .'

29. ibid., p. 61, ll. 1016-17.

30. In the speech of Electra in Act I beginning 'No aqueso, Fedra mía' we find the line 'de mi vida dudosa estrago cierto'; and two speeches further on zeugma in 'su intento y mi esperanza lleve el viento'.

31. Ignacio López de Ayala, *Numancia destruida. Tragedia* (Madrid, 1775), 'Asunto de esta tragedia'.

32. See *Obras de Cervantes Saavedra*, II, ed. F. Ynduráin, *BAE*, 156, p. xix.

33. López de Ayala, *Numancia destruida*, ed. cit., 'Dedicatoria'.

34. See N. Glendinning, *Vida y obra de Cadalso*, p. 43, and *BRAH*, CLXI, 2 (1967), 132.

35. See Archivo de la Secretaría, Madrid, 3-471-12.

36. *BAE*, 46, p. 59 b.

37. See Joaquín Arce, 'Rococó, Neoclasicismo y Prerromanticismo', in *El Padre Feijoo y su siglo*, II, 463.

38. See José Subirá, *El compositor Iriarte y el cultivo español del melólogo* (Barcelona, 1949-50).

39. See Albert Dérozier, op. cit., pp. 77 *et seq.*

40. *BAE*, 19, p. 42.

41. Ramón de la Cruz, *Sainetes*, ed. Cotarelo, II, *NBAE*, 26, p. 50b.

42. ibid., p. 50 a.

43. See above, p. 84.

44. See Cotarelo y Mori, Discurso preliminar, *Sainetes de Don Ramón de la Cruz*, I (Madrid, 1915), *NBAE*, 23, p. xix.

45. See, for example, *La avaricia castigada* (1761), ed. cit., p. 22; *La pragmática*, Primera Parte (1761), ibid., 35 *et seq.*; *Las damas finas* (1762), ibid., 68 *et seq.*; etc.

46. *Loa* que precedió la representación de la comedia de Don Pedro Calderón de la Barca intitulada *La vida es sueño*: en la cual entraron varios caballeros y oficiales de la Guarnición de Orán, en cuyo Coliseo se representó, in Huerta's *Obras poéticas* (Madrid, 1779), II, 92 *et seq.*

47. Tragedia nueva Alexandro [i.e. O'Reilly] sobre Africa. Su autor Don Gerónimo Grimaldi. Con Licencia del Rey Nro Señor. Año de 1775. Se hallará en las casas de Iriarte, Campo y compañia. Impresa a costa de la nación española y de la sangre de la nobleza. (*BNM*, MSS 18574 No. 10.)

48. See, for example, Galdós's *Don Ramón de la Cruz y su época* (*Obras completas*, VI, Madrid, 1951, 1453 *et seq*). Cotarelo surveys the fortunes of the author in his *Don Ramón de la Cruz y sus obras*.

49. See Hidehito Higashitani, 'Estructura de las cinco comedias originales de Moratín. Exposición, enredo y desenlace', *Segismundo*, III (1967), 134-60.

50. N. Glendinning, 'Moratín y el derecho', in *PSA*, 140, pp. 123-48.

51. Don Pedro has too often been identified as *the* 'voice of reason'. But the average middle-class theatregoer would identify more readily with Don Antonio. Don Pedro is made a rather isolated person, slightly pedantic, easily stirred to anger and therefore not an 'ideal' voice of reason.

52. See E. Cotarelo y Mori, *María del Rosario Fernández. La Tirana*, pp. 6, *et seq*. The instructions for Reynaud are in the Archivo de la Secretaría, Madrid, 2-459-23.

53. *Ensayo sobre el origen y naturaleza de las pasiones, del gesto y de la acción teatral*, con un discurso preliminar en defensa del ejercicio cómico escrito por D. Fermín Eduardo Zeglirscosac (Madrid, 1800). A more restrained handbook for actors was a translation from the French: *El arte del teatro en que se manifiesta los verdaderos principios de la declamación teatral* . . . traducido por D. Joseph de Resma (Madrid, 1783).

54. *BNM*, MSS 9587, p. 284.

55. Jorge Campos, *Teatro y sociedad* (1780-1820) (Madrid, 1969), pp. 30 *et seq*.

56. BM, Add. 33,478 f 2 *et seq*.

57. *Obras de D. Leandro Fernández de Moratín* (Madrid, 1830), II, 1. Quoted Campos, op. cit., p. 106.

58. Campos, op. cit., p. 92.

CODA

IN EUROPE AFTER THE FRENCH REVOLUTION freedom and equality were crucial topics. There was also a fear of these things. In literature we have seen how the century brought a liberation of the artist's imagination and a concern for the individual writer's personal vision. A backlash, or a revaluation of conventions, was equally inevitable in literature.

In 1808 Spanish intellectuals were confronted with an unenviable choice: to support an illiberal Spanish monarchy against the French invader, or to support the French monarch (Napoleon's brother José) in the hope of bringing about a new stability. Many on both sides hoped for a kind of revolution. Both sides had their inevitable share of patriots and opportunists, of opportunist patriots and patriotic opportunists.

Leandro Fernández de Moratín, who supported José Buonaparte, believed that a revolution was coming which would 'improve the nature of the monarchy, establishing it anew upon the solid foundations of reason, justice and power'. In the previous years the Spanish had been 'deceived by their magistrates, writers, aristocrats, political leaders and clergy', according to Moratín. He felt that a new Golden Age was imminent, when it would no longer be a crime to criticise 'shortcomings which were harmful to society'. On the other side liberals like Quintana watched hopefully over the *Cortes* meeting in Cadiz in 1811 as it drafted and debated a new constitution.

Ferdinand VII's restoration in 1814, the revival of the Inquisition, and the abandonment of the liberal constitution dashed many of these hopes. 'Truth is dead', wrote Goya as a caption for one of his *Disasters of War*. Would it rise again? he asked in another. The post-war period brought the supposedly liberal movement of Romanticism to Spain in its most reactionary form, idealising monarchical and aristocratic sentiments, as well as nationalistic and religious ones. Ironically, therefore, many Spanish liberals continued to prefer the Neo-classic aesthetic, which embodied an international spirit, even if it constituted a literary counterpart to absolutist regimes in origin. The war momentarily liberated, and then peace repressed. The 'varied, emotional, picturesque and sometimes daring' style which a reviewer found in Martínez de la Rosa's poem *Zaragoza* in 1811, 'inspiring all the passions at one and the same time and inflaming the imagination', had to wait some time for renewed expression.

Artistic differences at this period reflect a variety of training and temperamental inclinations as well as conflicting political views. There is no easy explanation of the trends; no simple pattern. At all periods there are those who surge forward and those who hold back. Some who broke new ground in literature were politically conservative. Some political radicals were pillars of the literary establishment.

Nowhere is this complexity more apparent than in attitudes to the imagination and originality. Originality can never seem a virtue to everyone. Ceán Bermúdez (1749-1829) felt that it verged on an undesirable distortion of nature, and did not wholly approve of it. Dr Johnson said of *Tristram Shandy*, 'Nothing odd will do long'. León de Arroyal, who was advanced in his political views, mocked originality in one of his *Epigramas* (Madrid, 1784), Book I, No. 65, in the following terms:

> A pregnant lady read a book
> whose worth, the author undertook,
> lay in originality,
> and she admired its quality.
> Later, when her time was done,
> she had a monster not a son,
> and instead of feeling sad,
> she said that she was very glad.
> 'Now I'm original! What joy
> not to have a girl or boy,
> a he or she but an it', she said,
> 'As good as the man whose book I read!'

Others opposed this rather Johnsonian line, welcoming the possibilities of greater freedom of expression which a less hierarchical society offered. As the tyranny of patrons declined, or the number of middle-class patrons increased, artists could more easily create what they wanted to create instead of satisfying someone else's demands.

Goya was one of the artists whose work changed radically as a result of this freedom. Particularly notable is his pursuit of the imagination in the last decade of the eighteenth century. In a letter to Bernardo de Iriarte (the brother of Tomás) in 1793, he revealed the keenness of this interest when he wrote about 'observations' he had made in a series of small paintings 'for which there is no opportunity in commissioned works, *which give no scope for fantasy and invention*'. Twenty-three years later, on the title-page of his *Tauromaquia* series of etchings, he proudly proclaimed himself an original artist ('pintor original'), and his friend Ceán Bermúdez praised his independent qualities. Goya's illness—and above all deafness—no doubt contributed to his sense of independence, yet his was not an isolated case. In the 1790s we find Jovellanos writing to José Vargas Ponce and encouraging him to show more individuality in what he writes. 'My friend', he says,

Nature has given every man a style, in the same way as she has given him facial features and character. A man can cultivate, polish and improve it, yet not change it. And no one who tries to do so will escape Nature's punishment. In my view, that is what has happened to you and to all those who have tried to get away from themselves, fleeing originality and giving themselves up to the imitation of others. Because you have done this you have come to seem other than you really are. You have read Mariana nine times over, Luis de León a hundred times, Cervantes a thousand, and I know not how many the person you call your master [i.e. Jovellanos himself]. In the long run, though you had the ability to beat us all, you ended up by being less than yourself . . . Recover your personality; write as you speak, compose as you write . . .

Such views were not unusual at the end of the century. Even the Real Academia de San Fernando, which often advocated the imitation of the great masters, criticised a late eighteenth-century building design on the grounds of lack of originality. Tensions between individual freedom and conventions played themselves out in style as well as in politics at this period. Sánchez Barbero, who suffered like many other liberals at the hands of Ferdinand VII's regime, wrote *Principios de retórica y poética* (Madrid, 1813) in which the passions and imagination of the individual were held to be the main sources of eloquence. Yet somehow the individual passions also had to be held in check. Goya expresses the dilemma with his own unique power in *Capricho* No. 43, 'El sueño de la razón produce monstruos'. On the one hand, imagination uncontrolled by reason gives rise to darkness and nightmare, while, on the other, allied with reason the imagination is the source of all the arts. Goya's originality in this particular etching, like that of all great artists in the eighteenth century, lay less in what he was saying than in the way in which he said it. We need not look far for the intolerance, political oppression, and social pressures Goya and his contemporaries faced. They still speak to us.

APPENDIX A

ANALYSIS OF SUBSCRIBERS' LISTS BY SOCIAL CLASS

THE FOLLOWING ANALYSIS is based on a simple division of the subscribers' lists into four categories: 1. those persons with titles or the style 'Excelentísimo Señor'; 2. those without title or style who are not clergy; 3. clergy and members of religious orders; and 4. libraries, institutions, and booksellers. The total number of subscribers in each category by my count follows that number expressed as a percentage of the whole.

Most subscription lists leave some cases open to doubt. Don Pedro de Silva is the son of a titled person but does not have a title himself. In the cases where I knew that a person styled simply 'Don' also had a title I counted him for the purpose of my analysis in Category 1. Not all lists distinguish priests by inserting the word 'presbítero' after the name. There are also a very few foreign subscribers in some lists which may distort the figures in a marginal way.

The decrease in the percentage of nobles in the population over the period should be borne in mind. An index of the decrease is given by the census figures for 1786, 1787, and 1797. The percentage of nobles in these was 7.2, 4.6, and 3.8 respectively.

The subscribers' list analyses come from the following books:

1. *Obras de Torres Villarroel*, 14 vols. (Salamanca, 1752), List in Vol. I = *A*.
2. ibid. List in Vol. 14. (Collated with Vol. I = *B*).
3. Juan de Yriarte, *Obras sueltas* (Madrid, 1774).
4. Lope de Vega, *Obras sueltas* (Madrid, 1776).
5. Pedro López de Ayala, *Crónicas de los reyes de Castilla*... Tomo I (Madrid, 1779).
6. *Crónica del Señor Rey Don Juan Segundo*... compilada por... Fernán Pérez de Guzmán (Valencia, 1779).
7. Antonio Valladares y Sotomayor, *Semanario erudito*, Vols. III and VI (Madrid, 1787) and Vol. IX (1788).
8. Tomás de Iriarte, *Colección de obras* (Madrid, 1787).

9. Antonio de Capmany, *Teatro histórico-crítico de la elocuencia española* (Madrid, 1786-98).
10. *Correo de los ciegos de Madrid*, Tomo II (Madrid, 1788); Tomo III, 1788, and Tomo IV, 1789.
11. Cervantes, *Don Quijote, con las notas de Pellicer* (Madrid, 1798).
12. Torres Villarroel, *Obras* (Madrid, 1794-99).
13. El P. F. Ramón Valvidares y Longo, *La Iberiada. Poema épico* (Cadiz, 1813).
14. Juan de Mariana, *Historia de España* (Madrid, 1817).

SUBSCRIBERS' LISTS

		Torres A 1752	Torres B 1752	Iriarte 1774	Lope 1776	Ayala 1779	P. de Guzmán 1779	Semanario erudito III 1787	Semanario erudito VI 1787	Semanario erudito IX 1788	Iriarte 1787	Capmany 1786–94	Correo II	Correo III 1788–89	Correo IV	Cervantes 1798	Torres 1799	Valvidares 1813	Mariana 1817
Titled	%	27.1	16.7	28.8	15.5	12.6	16.5	8.8	12	17.5	22.9	9.6	13.5	14.4	10.3	5.5	3	16	6.1
	number	76	83	40	34	52	55	22	38	55	128	14	41	28	26	29	15	40	54
Untitled	%	38	44.3	68.3	65.8	57.3	59	68.9	67.1	73.6	74.4	69.3	81.2	75.3	80.3	86.1	80.6	81.1	72.4
	number	102	209	95	144	236	197	171	212	231	415	101	247	146	203	452	404	202	626
Clergy	%	15.9	20.4	2.9	15.5	22.6	21.3	20.3	19	8.3	1.1	19.1	3.7	8.8	8.3	4.2	16.4	2.8	19
	number	43	100	4	34	93	71	50	58	26	6	28	11	17	21	22	82	7	166
Libraries	%	18	18.6		3.2	7.5	3.2	2	1.9	0.6	1.6	2	1.6	1.5	1.1	4.2			2.5
	number	49	91		7	31	11	5	6	2	9	3	5	3	3	22			23
Total per cent		100	100	100	100	100	100	100	100	100	100	100	100	100	100	100	100	100	100
Total subscribers		270	491	139	219	412	334	248	314	314	558	146	304	194	253	525	501	249	869
Total copies subscribed		270	491	141	219	431	406	281	369	347	692	146	320	219	268	704	652	249	921

APPENDIX B

BOOK PRICES IN THE EIGHTEENTH CENTURY

Date	Author Title	18th-c. price	Expressed new pence	Expressed $
1737	Luzán *Poética*	768 mˢ	(5/0¼d.)	25p 60 cents
1741	Lozano *Soledades de la vida*	288 mˢ	(1/1½d.)	6p 15 cents
1743	Torres Villarroel *Vida*	60 mˢ	(4½d.)	2p 5 cents
1754	Luis Joseph Velázquez *Orígenes de la poesía castellana*	184 mˢ	(1/0½d.)	5½p 13 cents
1758	Padre Isla *Fray Gerundio* Parte I	336 mˢ	(2/2½d.)	11½p 26¼ cents
	Feijoo, *Teatro crítico universal* Vol. 1	400 mˢ	(2/7¼d.)	13p 31¼ cents
	Vol. 8	404 mˢ	(2/7½d.)	13½p 32½ cents
1761	Rueda *Instrucción para grabar en cobre*	87 mˢ	(6d.)	2½p 6 cents
1765	*Montesquieu, *L'Esprit des lois*	127 rˢ	(£1 8s. 2d.)	£1.41 $3.38
	Feijoo, *Teatro crítico universal* and *Cartas eruditas*, 13 vols.	210 rˢ	(£2 6s. 6d.)	£2.32½ $5.58
1766	*Ercilla *Araucana*	22 rˢ	(4/4d.)	21½p 51½ cents
1769-78	*Parnaso español*, 9 vols.	135 rˢ	(£1 9s. 9d.)	£1.49 $3.58
1772	*Cadalso, *Los eruditos a la violeta*	21 rˢ	(4/7d.)	21p 50½ cents
	*Diderot, *Oeuvres philosophiques*, 6 vols.	100 rˢ	(£1 2s. 2d.)	£1.11 $2.66
1780	*Raynal, *Histoire philosophique... dans les deux Indes*, 11 vols.	500 rˢ	(£5 11s.)	£5.55 $13.32
1781	Cadalso, *Los eruditos a la violeta, Suplemento, Ocios de mi juventud*, and *Don Sancho García*	17 rˢ	(3/9d.)	18½p 44½ cents
	(price 'en pasta'; 'en rústica' cost 13 rˢ)			
1782-94	*Enciclopedia metódica*, Sancha, each vol.	60 rˢ	(13/2d.)	66p $1.59
	the set	200 rˢ	(£2 4s.)	£2.20 $5.28
1774	*Locke *Essai ... l'entendement humain*	74 rˢ	(16/3d.)	81p $1.94
	*Helvétius, *Oeuvres*, 4 vols.	170 rˢ	(£1 16s. 2d.)	£1.81 $4.34

Date	Author Title	18th-c. price	Expressed new pence	Expressed $
1774	*Hume, *Discours politiques*, 2 vols.	32 rˢ	(7/2d.)	36p 90 cents
	*Rousseau, *Oeuvres complètes*, 11 vols.	440 rˢ (£4 17s. 6d.)	£4.87½	$11.70
1817	Capmany, *Cuestiones críticas* (en pasta)	20 rˢ	(4/2d.)	21p 50½ cents
	Isla, *Cartas familiares*, 6 vols. (en pasta)	60 rˢ	(12/6d.)	62½p $1.50
	Montengón, *El Eusebio*, 4 vols.	24 rˢ	(5/-)	25p 60 cents
	Biblioteca universal de novelas, cuentos e historias instructivas y agradables			
	Vol. IV (en pasta)	14 rˢ	(2/10d.)	14p 33½ cents
	(en rústica)	11 rˢ	(2/1d.)	10½p 25 cents
	To subscribers to series (en pasta)	12 rˢ	(2/6d.)	12½p 30 cents
	(en rústica)	9 rˢ	(1/8¼d.)	8½p 20½ cents
	Cost in provinces involves increase of	1 r	(2¼d.)	1p 2½ cents

Note. The prices of books marked with an asterisk are strictly speaking valuations made in 1782 and the price may have been different; they are taken from Georges Demerson, *Don Juan Meléndez Valdés et son temps* (Paris, 1962), pp. 61 *et seq.* There must have been some variations in prices of foreign books. But it is worth recording that whereas Meléndez Valdés valued his Helvétius at 170 *reales*, the University of Salamanca spent 25 *reales* on a five-volume edition in 1787 (cf. Demerson, op. cit., p. 115), i.e. about 4/10d. in English money of the period instead of £1 16s. 2d. On the other hand, Meléndez's valuation of his Spanish books seems far from inflated. The 1758 Feijoo edition, which has a *tasa* price in Vols. 1 and 8, must have cost about £1 13s. 7d. for thirteen vols.; Meléndez's copy of the 1765 edition is only valued at £2 6s. 6d., and the later edition would probably have cost rather more in any case. To get some idea of the equivalent price today eighteenth-century prices should be multiplied by between 10 and 15.

APPENDIX C

FREQUENCY OF EIGHTEENTH-CENTURY EDITIONS

Author and Work	Number of Editions				
	1700-29	1730-49	1750-69	1770-99	1800-20
Cervantes, *Quijote*	7	8	8	12	14
Novelas ejemplares	3	8	1	4	6
Feijoo, *Teatro crítico*	–	2	2	6	–
Gracián, *Criticón*	5	4	1	2	–
Lazarillo de Tormes	2	1	1	1	7
Lozano, *Soledades de la vida*	6	3	1	2	1
Luis de Granada, *Libro de oración*	7	3	11	20	10
Quevedo, *Sueños*	7	–	1	15	–
Torres Villarroel, *Sueños*	1	–	3	4	–
Gil Polo, *Diana enamorada*	–	1	–	1	2

This table shows the rises and falls in the popularity of Quevedo and Gracián which took place during the eighteenth century. Other sixteenth-century writers' fortunes are also tabulated, and Feijoo is included to show the extent to which contemporary writers competed with those of earlier periods; though there is a marked decline in favour (or influence) of Gracián, which parallels rising opposition to the more elaborate styles in the second half of the century.

APPENDIX D

ANALYSIS OF EIGHTEENTH-CENTURY PUBLICATIONS BY SUBJECT

The following table sets out the results of a very subjective analysis of the books and periodicals whose publication was announced in the *Gaceta de Madrid* in 1730, 1760, 1790, and 1815. The figures for the last three years are my own. Those for 1730 were kindly provided by Mrs Carmen Benjamin, a research student of King's College, London. The table should not be taken as more than a rough guide to probable trends. The survey did not conform with all the prerequisities for scientific testing, and it is clear that a research team will have to undertake a more detailed and year-by-year investigation before developments can be plotted with entire confidence. On the basis of the figures given below we infer that there was a striking rise in the total output of the Spanish presses between 1730 and 1815. The fall-off in the final year is probably due to the fact that the Peninsular War had only just ended. Over the period as a whole the decline of religious publications seems marked, and printings of Greek and Latin authors also fell. On the other hand, educational, legal, and historical or geographical publications increase, and so does the output of works of literature in prose. Although poetry appears to fall, occasional poems published in 1760—which was the first full year of Charles III's reign—may well have distorted the figures slightly. Scientific and agricultural publications do not rise as much as might be expected. Yet economic and commercial books make the significant start in the second half of the century which one would have assumed.

Subject	Volumes published				Percentages			
	1730	1760	1790	1816	1730	1760	1790	1815
Art	—	1	2	5	—	0.63	0.36	1.16
Economics/Commerce	—	—	19	10	—	—	3.45	2.33
Education	5	9	31	35	4.76	5.7	5.64	8.17
Greek and Latin authors	—	7	10	4	—	4.43	1.82	0.93

History/Geography	4	13	28	43	3.8	8.22	5.09	10.04
Law	1	4	15	13	0.95	2.53	2.72	3.03
Literature								
(i) Poetry	—	8	12	14	—	5.06	2.18	3.27
(ii) Prose	7	8	47	44	6.66	5.06	8.55	10.28
(iii) Drama	—	8	37	15	—	5.06	6.73	3.5
(iv) Criticism/ Polemic	—	1	16	9	—	0.63	2.91	2.11
Military	—	4	5	32	—	2.53	0.91	7.47
Moral/Philosophical	—	4	12	5	—	2.53	2.18	1.16
Periodicals	12	21	58	9	11.42	13.29	10.55	2.1
Politics	2	5	37	23	1.90	3.16	6.61	5.37
Religious	55	44	148	96	52.38	28.48	26.9	22.42
Scientific/Agricultural	15	18	68	68	14.28	11.39	12.36	15.88
Miscellaneous	4	2	3	—	3.8	1.26	0.55	—
Totals	105	158	550	428				

SELECT BIBLIOGRAPHY

1. *The Enlightenment in Spain and Political and Religious Institutions*

F. Aguilar Piñal, *La Sevilla de Olavide (1767-1778)* (Seville, 1966)

G. Anés, *Economía e 'Ilustración en la España del siglo XVIII* (Barcelona, 1969)

M. Artola, *Los afrancesados* (Madrid, 1953)

——, *Los orígenes de la España contemporánea* (Madrid, 1959)

——, 'Asturias en la etapa final del antiguo régimen', in *El Padre Feijoo y su siglo*, *CCF*, 18 (1966), I, 135-52

R. Carande, *El 'despotismo ilustrado' de los Amigos del País* (Bilbao, 1957)

R. Carr, *Spain 1808-1939* (Oxford, 1966)

J. E. Casariego, *El marqués de Sargadelos o los comienzos del industrialismo capitalista en España* (Oviedo, 1950)

C. E. Corona Baratech, *Revolución y reacción en el reinado de Carlos IV* (Madrid, 1957)

M. Defourneaux, 'Tradition et lumières dans le "despotismo ilustrado"', in *Utopie et Institutions au XVIIIe siècle* (Paris-Le Haye, 1963), pp. 229-45.

G. Demerson, *La Real Sociedad de Amigos del País de Avila* (Avila, 1968)

——, *La Real Sociedad Económica de Valladolid (1784-1808)* (Valladolid, 1969)

A. Domínguez Ortiz, *La sociedad española en el siglo XVIII* (Madrid, 1955)

A. Elorza, *La ideología liberal en la Ilustración española* (Madrid, 1970)

R. Herr, *The Eighteenth-Century Revolution in Spain* (Princeton, 1958)

J. Marías, *La España posible en tiempo de Carlos III* (Estudios de humanidades, 1, Madrid, 1963)

A. Mestre Sanchís, *Ilustración y reforma de la Iglesia. Pensamiento político religioso de Don Gregorio Mayáns y Siscar (1699-1781)* Valencia, 1968)

R. Olaechea, 'Anotaciones sobre la inmunidad local en el siglo XVIII español', *Miscelánea Comillas*, XLVI (1966), 295-381
——, *Las relaciones hispano-romanas en la segunda mitad del siglo XVIII. La agencia de preces* (Saragossa, 1965)
V. Palacio Atard, *Los españoles de la Ilustración* (Madrid, 1964)
V. Rodríguez Casado, *La política y los políticos en el reinado de Carlos III* (Madrid, 1962)
——, 'La administración pública en el reinado de Carlos III, *CCF*, 12 (1961)
L. Sánchez Agesta, *El pensamiento político del despotismo ilustrado* (Madrid, 1953)
——, 'España y Europa en el pensamiento español del siglo XVIII', *CCF*, 2 (1955)
J. Sarrailh, *L'Espagne éclairée de la seconde moitié du XVIIIe siècle* (Paris, 1954)
J. Saugnieux, *Un Prélat éclairé. Don Antonio Tavira y Almazán (1737-1807). Contribution à l'étude du Jansénisme espagnol* (Toulouse, 1970)
——, 'Un Janséniste modéré: José Climent, évêque de Barcelone', *BH*, LXX (1968), 468-75
P. Vilar, 'Structures de la société espagnole vers 1750', *Mélanges à la mémoire de Jean Sarrailh* (Paris, 1966), II, 425-47
J. Urquijo, *Los Amigos del País (según cartas y otros documentos inéditos del XVIII)* (San Sebastián, 1929)

2. *Education, and Cultural Institutions*

G. M. Addy, *The Enlightenment in the University of Salamanca* (Durham, 1966)
F. Aguilar Piñal, *Los comienzos de la crisis universitaria en España* (Madrid, 1967)
——, *La universidad de Sevilla en el siglo XVIII. Estudio sobre la primera reforma universitaria moderna* (Anales de la Universidad hispalense, serie Filosofía y Letras, 1, Madrid, 1969)
Á. González Palencia, 'Notas sobre la enseñanza del francés a fines del siglo XVIII y principios del XIX, in *Eruditos y libreros del siglo XVIII* (Madrid, 1948), 419-27
——, 'La primera enseñanza en los principios del siglo XIX', in *Entre dos siglos* (Madrid, 1943), 335-47.
A. Marcos Montero, 'El magisterio en la época de Carlos III', *Revista Española de Pedagogía*, 12 (1954), 497-506
J. M. Ruiz, 'La primera acción literaria de la Academia de la Historia', *BBMP*, 46 (1968), 71-102

L. Sala Balust, *Visitas y reforma de los Colegios Mayores de Salamanca en el reinado de Carlos III* (Valladolid, 1958)

J. Simón Díaz, *Historia del Colegio Imperial de Madrid* (Madrid, 1959)

3. *Book-publication, Censorship and the Inquisition*

M. Defourneaux, *L'Inquisition espagnole et les livres français au XVIIIe siècle* (Paris, 1963)

T. Egido López, *Prensa clandestina española del siglo XVIII: 'El Duende crítico'* (Valladolid, 1968)

L. M. Enciso Recio, *La Gaceta de Madrid y el Mercurio Histórico y Político, 1756–1781* (Valladolid, 1957)

——, *Nipho y el periodismo español del siglo XVIII* (Valladolid, 1956)

Á. González Palencia, 'Joaquín Ibarra y el juzgado de imprentas', in *Eruditos y libreros del siglo XVIII*, 313–63

A. Rodríguez-Moñino, 'El *Quijote* de Don Antonio de Sancha' in *Relieves de erudición* (Madrid, 1959), pp. 277–88

——, *Historia de los catálogos de librería españoles (1661–1840)* (Madrid, 1966)

A. Rumeu de Armas, *Historia de la censura gubernativa en España* (Madrid, 1940)

M. Serrano y Sanz, 'El Consejo de Castilla y la censura de libros en el siglo XVIII', *RBAM*, XV (1906), 28–46, 242–59, 387–402; XVI (1907), 108–16 and 206–18.

4. *Literary Theory, Aesthetics, Language, and Cultural Contact*

R. Andioc, *Sur la querelle du théâtre au temps de Leandro Fernández de Moratín* (Bordeaux, 1970)

J. Arce, N. Glendinning, and L. Dupuis, 'La literatura española del siglo XVIII y sus fuentes extranjeras', *CCF*, 20 (1968)

J. Arce, 'Rococó, Neoclasicismo y Prerromanticismo en la poesía española del siglo XVIII', in *El Padre Feijoo y su siglo, CCF*, 18 (1966), II, 447–77

M. Batllori, 'Las relaciones culturales hispano-francesas en el siglo XVIII', *Cuadernos de historia: anexos de la Revista Hispania*, 2 (Madrid, 1968), 205–49

J. Campos, *Teatro y sociedad en España (1780–1820)* (Estudios de humanidades, 7, Madrid, 1969)

J. L. Cano, 'Una "Poética" desconocida del XVIII. Las "reflexiones sobre la poesía" de N. Philoaletheias (1787)', *BH*, LXIII (1961), 62–87

J. Caso González, J. Arce, and J. Gaya Nuño, 'Los conceptos de rococó, neoclasicismo y prerromanticismo en la literatura española del siglo XVIII', *CCF*, 22 (1970)

J. A. Cook, *Neo-Classic Drama in Spain. Theory and Practice* (Dallas, 1959)

M. Cruz Seoane, *El primer lenguaje constitucional español* (*Las Cortes de Cádiz*) (Estudios de humanidades, 5, Madrid, 1968)

M. Defourneaux, *Pablo de Olavide ou l'Afrancesado (1725–1803)* (Paris, 1959)

G. Delpy, *L'Espagne et l'esprit européen: l'oeuvre de Feijoo* (Paris, 1936)

M. Durán, 'Jovellanos, Moratín y Goya. Una nueva interpretación del siglo XVIII español', *CA*, 34 (1965), 193–8

N. Glendinning, 'La fortuna de Góngora en el siglo XVIII', *RFE*, XLIV, 1961 (1963), 323–49

E. F. Helman, *Trasmundo de Goya* (Madrid, 1963)

R. Lapesa, 'Ideas y palabras: del vocabulario de la Ilustración al de los primeros liberales', *Asclepio*, 18–19 (1966–67), 189–218

F. Lázaro Carreter, *Las ideas lingüísticas en España durante el siglo XVIII* (Madrid, 1949)

I. L. McClelland, *The Origins of the Romantic Movement in Spain* (Liverpool, 1937)

——, 'The Eighteenth-Century Conception of the Stage and Histrionic Technique', in *Estudios hispánicos. Homenaje a Archer M. Huntington* (Wellesley, 1952), pp. 393–425

——, *Spanish Drama of Pathos 1750–1808* (Liverpool, 1970)

M. Menéndez y Pelayo, *Historia de las ideas estéticas en España*, ed. E. Sánchez Reyes, in *Obras completas* (Santander, 1947), III: *Siglo XVIII*

P. Mérimée, *L'Influence française en Espagne au dix-huitième siècle* (Paris, 1936)

E. Orozco, 'Porcel y el barroquismo literario del siglo XVIII', *CCF*, 21 (1968)

R. E. Pellissier, *The Neo-Classic Movement in Spain during the XVIIIth Century* (Leland Stanford Junior University Publications, University Series, 29–35, Stanford, 1918)

J. de la Puente, *La visión de la realidad española en los viajes de Don Antonio Ponz* (Estudios de humanidades, 6, Madrid, 1968)

C. Real de la Riva, 'La escuela poética salmantina del siglo XVIII', *BBMP*, XXIV (1948), 321–64

R. P. Sebold, 'Contra los mitos anti-neoclásicos españoles', *PS.4*, 103 (1964), 83–114

J. Sempere y Guarinos, *Ensayo de una biblioteca española de los mejores escritores del reinado de Carlos III* (Madrid, 1785–89; facsimile reprint, 6 vols. in 3, Madrid, 1969)

Marqués de Valmar (L. A. Cueto), 'Bosquejo histórico crítico de la poesía castellana en el siglo XVIII', *BAE*, 61 (Madrid, 1869 and other eds.)

5. Principal Authors

Arteaga
E. de Arteaga, *La belleza ideal*, ed. M. Batllori, CC 122 (Madrid, 1943)

Cadalso
José Cadalso, *Los eruditos a la violeta*, ed. N. Glendinning (Salamanca—Madrid—Barcelona—Caracas, 1968)

——, *Cartas marruecas*, ed. L. Dupuis and N. Glendinning (London, 1966)

——, *Defensa de la nación española contra la Carta persiana LXXVIII de Montesquieu*, ed. G. Mercadier (Toulouse, 1970)

——, *Noches lúgubres*, ed. E. F. Helman (Madrid, 1968)

——, *Noches lúgubres*, ed. N. Glendinning, CC 152 (Madrid, 1961)

M. Baquero Goyanes, 'Perspectivismo y crítica en Cadalso, Larra y Mesonero Romanos', in *Perspectivismo y contraste (de Cadalso a Pérez de Ayala)* (Madrid, 1963)

A. Ferrari, 'Las "Apuntaciones autobiográficas" de José de Cadalso en un tomo de "Varios" ', *BRAH*, CLXI (1967), 111–43

N. Glendinning, *Vida y obra de Cadalso* (Madrid, 1962)

J. Marichal, 'Cadalso: el estilo de un "hombre de bien" ', in *La voluntad de estilo* (Barcelona, 1957)

B. W. Wardropper, 'Cadalso's *Noches lúgubres* and Literary Tradition', *SPh*, XLIX (1952)

Capmany
M. Baquero Goyanes, 'Prerromanticismo y retórica: Antonio de Capmany', in *Studia philologica. Homenaje ofrecido a Dámaso Alonso* (Madrid, 1960), I, 171–89

N. Glendinning, 'A Note on the Authorship of the *Comentario sobre el Doctor Festivo y Maestro de los Eruditos a la Violeta para desengaño de los españoles que leen poco y malo*', *BHS*, XLIII (1966), 276–83

Cienfuegos

N. Álvarez de Cienfuegos, *Poesías*, BAE, 67 (Madrid, 1875 and later eds.)

——, *Poesías*, ed. J. L. Cano (Madrid, CCa, 1969)

J. L. Cano, 'Cienfuegos y la amistad', *Clavileño*, 34 (1955), 35–40

——, 'Cienfuegos, poeta social', *PSA*, 6 (1957), 248–70

R. Froldi, 'Natura e società nell' opera di Cienfuegos', *ACME, Annali della Facoltà di Lettere e Filosofia degli Studi*, XXI, 1 (Milan, 1968)

A. Mas, 'Cienfuegos y le Prérromantisme européen', *Mélanges à la mémoire de Jean Sarrailh* (Paris, 1966), II

Clavijo y Fajardo

J. Clavijo y Fajardo, *El pensador* (Madrid, 1762–67), extracts in *Costumbristas españoles*, ed. E. Correa Calderón (Madrid, 1950)

Ramón de la Cruz

R. de la Cruz, *Sainetes*, ed. E. Cotarelo y Mori, 2 vols., *NBAE*, 23, 26 (Madrid, 1915–28)

E. Cotarelo y Mori, *Don Ramón de la Cruz y sus obras* (Madrid, 1899)

Feijoo

Benito Jerónimo Feijoo, *Obras escogidas*, BAE, 56, 141, 142 (various editions)

——, *Teatro crítico universal*, ed. A. Millares Carlo, CC 48, 53, 67 (Madrid, 1923–25 and later eds.)

——, *Cartas eruditas*, ed. A. Millares Carlo, CC 85 (Madrid, 1928 and later eds.)

A. Ardao, *La filosofía polémica de Feijoo* (Buenos Aires, 1962)

G. Delpy, *L'Espagne et l'esprit européen: l'oeuvre de Feijoo* (Paris, 1936)

El Padre Feijoo y su siglo, a collection of studies, 3 vols., *CCF*, 18 (1966)

G. Marañón, *Las ideas biológicas del padre Feijoo*, 4th ed. (Madrid, 1962) and in BAE, 141, pp. xi-clxv

J. Marichal, 'Feijoo y su papel de desengañador de las Españas', in *La voluntad de estilo* (Barcelona, 1957), pp. 165–84

I. L. McClelland, *Benito Jerónimo Feijoo* (New York, 1969)

R. Lapesa, 'Sobre el estilo de Feijoo' in *De la edad media a nuestros días* (Madrid, 1967), pp. 290–9

SELECT BIBLIOGRAPHY 143

Fernández de Moratín, Leandro
Leandro Fernández de Moratín, *Obras, BAE,* 2 (Madrid, 1846 and later eds.)
——, *Obras póstumas,* 3 vols. (Madrid, 1867)
——, *La comedia nueva,* ed. J. C. Dowling (Madrid, 1970)
——, *La comedia nueva y El sí de las niñas,* ed. J. C. Dowling and R. Andioc (Madrid, CCa, 1968)
——, *Diario (1780–1808),* ed. R. and M. Andioc (Madrid, 1968)
J. Casalduero, 'Forma y sentido de *El sí de las niñas*', *NRFH,* XI (1957), 36–56
N. Glendinning, 'Moratín y el derecho', *PSA,* 140 (1967), 125–48
H. Higashitani, 'Estructura de las cinco comedias originales de Moratín. Exposición, enredo y desenlace', *Segismundo,* III (1967), 134–60
Insula, XV, No. 161 (1960). Special number with articles on Moratín
Revista de la Universidad de Madrid, IX, No. 35 (1969): *Moratín y la sociedad española de su tiempo*

Fernández de Moratín, Nicolás
Nicolás Fernández de Moratín, *Obras, BAE,* 2 (Madrid, 1846 and later eds.)
——, *Arte de las putas* (Madrid, 1898)
E. F. Helman, 'The Elder Moratín and Goya', *HR,* XXIII (1955), 219–30

Forner
Juan Pablo Forner, *Poesías, BAE,* 63 (Madrid, 1871 and later eds.)
——, *El asno erudito. Fábula original,* ed. M. Muñoz Cortés (Valencia, 1948)
——, *Cotejo de las églogas que ha premiado la Real Academia Española,* ed. F. Lázaro Carreter (Salamanca, 1951)
——, *Los gramáticos, historia chinesca,* ed. J. H. R. Polt (Madrid, 1970)
——, *Obras escogidas y ordenadas por Don Luis Villanueva* (Madrid, 1844)
M. Jiménez Salas, *Vida y obras de Don Juan Pablo Forner y Segarra* (Madrid, 1944)

Huerta
Vicente García de la Huerta, *Raquel,* ed. J. G. Fucilla (Salamanca—Madrid—Barcelona, 1965)
——, *Raquel,* ed R. Andioc (Madrid, CCa, 1971)

Iglesias

José Iglesias de la Casa, *Poesías, BAE,* 61 (Madrid, 1869 and later eds.)

R. P. Sebold, 'Dieciochismo, estilo místico y contemplación en "La esposa aldeana" de Iglesias de la Casa', *PSA,* 146 (1968), 119-44

Iriarte

Tomás de Iriarte, *Poesías, BAE,* 63 (Madrid, 1875 and other eds.)

——, *Colección de obras en verso y prosa,* 6 vols. (Madrid, 1787); 8 vols. (Madrid, 1805)

——, *Poesías,* ed. A. Navarro González, CC 136 (Madrid, 1953)

E. Cotarelo y Mori, *Iriarte y su época* (Madrid, 1897)

R. P. Sebold, 'Tomás de Iriarte, poeta de "rapto racional" ', *CCF,* 11 (1961)

Isla

P. José Francisco de Isla, *Fray Gerundio de Campazas,* ed. R. P. Sebold, 4 vols., CC 148-51 (Madrid, 1960-64)

——, *Cartas inéditas,* ed. L. Fernández (Madrid, 1957)

B. Gaudeau, *Les prêcheurs burlesques en Espagne au XVIIIᵉ siècle. Étude sur le P. Isla* (Paris, 1891)

Jovellanos

Gaspar Melchor de Jovellanos, *Obras, BAE,* 46, 50 (Madrid, 1858-59 and later eds.) and *BAE,* 85, 86, and 87 (Madrid, 1956). Vols. 3-5 contain an especially valuable introduction

——, *Obras en Prosa,* ed. J. Caso González (Madrid, CCa, 1969)

——, *Obras, I: Epistolario,* ed. J. Caso González (Textos hispánicos modernos, 8, Barcelona, 1970)

——, *Obras escogidas,* ed. A. del Río, 3 vols., CC 110, 111, and 129 (Madrid, 1935-46)

——, *Poesías,* ed. J. Caso González (Oviedo, 1961)

J. Caso González, 'El delincuente honrado, drama sentimental', *Archivum,* XIV (1964), 103-33.

——, 'Escolásticos e inovadores a finales del siglo XVIII', *PSA,* 109 (1965), 25-48

E. F. Helman, ' "Sátira" sobre teatro y toros de Jovellanos', *PSA,* 157 (1969), 9-30

J. H. R. Polt, *Jovellanos and his English Sources* (Transactions of the American Philosophical Society, Vol. 54, part 7, Philadelphia, 1964)

——, 'Jovellanos y la educación', *El Padre Feijoo y su siglo*, *CCF*, 18 (1966), II, 315-38

R. Vergnes, 'Dirigisme et libéralisme économique à la Sociedad Económica de Madrid (De l'influence de Jovellanos)', *BH*, LXX (1969), 300-41

I. M. Zavala, 'Jovellanos y la poesía burguesa', *NRFH*, XVIII (1968), 47-64

Lista

Alberto Lista, *Poesías, BAE*, 67 (Madrid, 1875 and later eds.)

H. Juretschke, *Vida, obra y pensamiento de Alberto Lista* (Madrid, 1951)

Luzán

Ignacio de Luzán, *La Poética*, ed. L. de Filippo, 2 vols. (Barcelona, 1956)

——, *Memorias literarias de París* (Madrid, 1751)

R. P. Sebold, 'A Statistical Analysis of the Origins and Nature of Luzán's Ideas on Poetry', *HR, XXXV* (1967), 227-51

Meléndez Valdés

——, *Poesías, BAE*, 63 (Madrid, 1875 and other eds.)

——, *Poesías*, ed. P. Salinas, CC 64 (Madrid, 1925 and other eds.)

——, *Los besos de amor*, ed. R. Foulché-Delbosc, *RH*, I (1894)

——, *Discursos forenses* (Madrid, 1821)

——, *Poesías inéditas*, ed. A. Rodríguez-Moñino (Madrid, 1964)

W. E. Colford, *Juan Meléndez Valdés. A Study in the Transition from Neo-classicism to Romanticism in Spanish Poetry* (New York, 1942)

G. Demerson, *Don Juan Meléndez Valdés et son temps* (Paris, 1962)

——, *Don Juan Meléndez Valdés. Correspondance relative à la reunion des Hôpitaux d'Avila* (Bordeaux, 1964)

R. Froldi, *Un poeta illuminista: Meléndez Valdés* (Milan, 1967)

A. Forcione, 'Meléndez Valdés and the "Essay on Man"', *HR*, XXXIV (1966)

A. Rodríguez-Moñino, *Relieves de erudición* (Madrid, 1959), 291-310

Montengón

Á González Palencia, 'Pedro Montengón y su novela "El Eusebio"', *Entre dos siglos*, pp. 137–80

Montiano y Luyando

Agustín Montiano y Luyando, *Discursos sobre las tragedias españolas.*

6 * *

Virginia. Lucrecia, 2 vols. (Madrid, 1750-53)
Marqués de Laurencin, *Don Agustín Montiano y Luyando* (Madrid, 1926)

Mor de Fuentes
José Mor de Fuentes, *La Serafina*, ed. I.-M. Gil (Saragossa, 1959)
——, *Bosquejillo de su vida y escritos*, ed. M. Alvar (Granada, 1952)

Nipho
L. Enciso Recio, *Nipho y el periodismo español del siglo XVIII* (Valladolid, 1956)
P. J. Guinard, 'Un journaliste espagnol du XVIIIᵉ siècle: Francisco Mariano Nifo', *BH*, LIX (1957), 262-83

Porcel
J. A. Porcel y Salablanca, *Poesías, BAE*, 61 (Madrid, 1869 and later eds.)
E. Orozco, 'Porcel y el barroquismo literario del siglo XVIII', *CCF*, 21 (1968)

Quintana
Manuel José Quintana, *Poesías*, ed. N. Alonso Cortés, CC 78 (Madrid 1937)
——, *Poesías*, ed. A. Dérozier (Madrid, CCa, 1969)
A. Dérozier, *Manuel Josef Quintana et la naissance du libéralisme en Espagne* (Annales littéraires de l'Université de Besançon, 95, 2 vols., Paris, 1968-70)
R. P. Sebold, ' "Siempre formas en grande modeladas". Sobre la visión poética de Quintana', in *Homenaje a Rodríguez-Moñino. Estudios de erudición que le ofrecen sus amigos o discípulos hispanistas norteamericanos* (Madrid, 1966), II, 177-84

Samaniego
Félix María Samaniego, *Poesías, BAE*, 61 (Madrid, 1869 and later eds.)
——, *Fábulas*, ed. E. Jareño (Madrid, CCa, 1969)

Torrepalma
Alfonso Verdugo y Castilla, conde de Torrepalma, *Poesías, BAE*, 61 (Madrid, 1869 and later eds.)
N. Marín, 'La obra poética del Conde de Torrepalma', *CCF*, 15 (1964)

Torres Villarroel

Diego de Torres Villarroel, *Vida*, ed. F. de Onis (Madrid, CC, 1912 and later eds.)

——, *Visiones y visitas de Torres con Don Francisco de Quevedo por la corte*, ed R. P. Sebold, CC 161 (Madrid, 1966)

P. Ilie, 'Grotesque portraits in Torres Villarroel', *BHS*, XLV (1968), 16–37

R. P. Sebold, 'Torres Villarroel y las vanidades del mundo; *Archivum*, VII (1957), 115–46

——, 'Mixtificación y estructura picarescas en la "Vida" de Torres Villarroel', *Insula*, 204 (1963), 7 and 12

——, 'Torres Villarroel, Quevedo y El Bosco', *Insula*, 159 (1960), 3 and 14

INDEX

Printed in Great Britain by
The Garden City Press Limited, Letchworth, Hertfordshire, SG6 1JS

THE EIGHTEENTH CENTURY saw radical social and political change (though not revolution) in Spain. Traditional beliefs in Church and State; the assumptions of art, religion, and politics, were increasingly questioned by a minority in Spain as elsewhere in Europe. The country moved from absolutism through benevolent despotism, to a liberal constitution, and the backlash of absolutism. Spanish art and literature reflect the affirmations and uncertainties, the hopes and fears, of those living in troubled times.

PROFESSOR GLENDINNING EXAMINES the various forces influencing Spanish writers of the period and their reactions to foreign and national views of Spanish culture. He gives special attention to the composition and preferences of the eighteenth-century Spanish reading public.

IN HIS SURVEY of prose he traces the continuation of seventeenth-century literary traditions in Torres Villarroel, for example, and evaluates the works of innovators like Feijoo, Isla, Cadalso, and the exponents of 'impassioned argumentation', Jovellanos and Forner. Poetry reflects the change from the followers of Góngora earlier in the